D0284369

ARTEMIS

Other Books by Jean Shinoda Bolen

The Tao of Psychology

Goddesses in Everywoman

Gods in Everyman

Ring of Power

Crossing to Avalon

Close to the Bone

The Millionth Circle

Goddesses in Older Women

Crones Don't Whine

Urgent Message From Mother

Like a Tree

Moving Toward the Millionth Circle

Jean Shinoda Bolen, M.D.

Artemis

The Indomitable Spirit in Everywoman

Conari Press

First published in 2014 by Conari Press, an imprint of
Red Wheel/Weiser, llc

With offices at:
665 Third Street, Suite 400
San Francisco, CA 94107
www.redwheelweiser.com

ISBN: 978-1-57324-591-3

Library of Congress Cataloging-in-Publication Data available upon request.

Cover design by Jim Warner
Cover photograph: Artemis the Huntress (oil on panel), Fontainebleau School, (16th century) / Louvre, Paris, France / The Bridgeman Art Library
Interior by Maureen Forys, Happenstance Type-O-Rama
Typeset in Adobe Caslon Pro and Trajan Pro

Printed in the United States of America
EBM

10 9 8 7 6 5 4 3 2 1

For women and girls who identify with Artemis.
For girls who admire Artemis in others
and find this archetype is their growing edge.
For women in whom Artemis may be a late-blooming archetype.
For all who discover the indomitable spirit in themselves.
Or has loved it in someone else.

Contents

Introduction: The Indomitable Spirit in Everywoman ix

1. Atalanta the Myth 1

2. Atalanta, Artemis, Mother Bear 13

3. Atalanta and Meleager 39

4. The Hunt of the Calydon Boar 51

5. Atalanta in the Wilderness 69

6. The Footrace and the Three Golden Apples 93

7. Virgin Goddess Archetype: Artemis, Athena, Hestia 119

8. Goddesses of the Moon: Artemis/Selene/Hecate 153

9. Free to Be You and Me 183

Parting Thoughts 217

Resources 223

About the Author 235

Index 237

Introduction

The Indomitable Spirit in Everywoman

(Latin in + domitare: to tame; incapable of being subdued or tamed)

Indomitable spirit is an attribute in women who have Artemis as an active archetype. In mythology, Artemis is the Greek Goddess of the Hunt and Moon, known as Diana to the Romans. She was the first-born twin sister to Apollo the God of the Sun. As goddess of the hunt, she roamed the wilderness, armed with a bow and quiver of arrows, accompanied by her hunting dogs, either alone or with her chosen nymph companions. Artemis came to the rescue of her mother, was the protector of pre-pubescent girls and young animals. Pregnant women prayed to her to relieve them from pain. (*Artemisia*—the herb that bears her name, is used by midwives for this). She reacted swiftly to help those under her protection and to punish those who would harm them or disrespect her. Artemis is an archetypal predisposition toward egalitarian-brotherly relationships with men, a sense of sisterhood with women, the ability to aim for a distant target or rise to a challenge, and a preference to be in nature rather than cities.

Artemis: The Indomitable Spirit in Everywoman is a coming-full-circle book. I go back to the story of Atalanta that led me to write *Goddesses in Everywoman: A New Psychology of Women*, a book that initially became an unexpected best-seller, then a classic, celebrated by the publication of its thirtieth anniversary edition in 2014. It began as an entirely different book about two paths of feminine development with the working title *Pathways to Wholeness.* It was based on Greek myths about Psyche and Atalanta, two mortal women, one identified with Aphrodite, the other with Artemis.

In Jungian literature, the myth of Psyche is the model for the psychological development of the feminine psyche. While it does apply to many women, to say that this was the pattern for all women did not ring true for me. Psyche was the mortal woman who offended Aphrodite. Pregnant and abandoned by her lover, she tries to drown herself and finds she cannot. She then is given four tasks to complete and is initially overwhelmed by each task. Symbolic helpers then come to her rescue (each represents an inner resource that she did not know she has) and as the tasks are done, she grows psychologically. I wanted to find another myth that would apply to women who took on challenges, ventured into new fields, defined themselves, and who entered occupations and professions that had traditionally been male stronghold—women who were at ease with men as friends and equals. I found Atalanta.

My focus expanded after I wondered: What about the other Greek goddesses? And then, as if in response to this question, Hera, Goddess of Marriage, "appeared" in the psyche of a woman who had been taken over by Hera in her jealous aspect. My interest shifted to the major goddesses in *Goddesses in Everywoman.* As a result, only remnants of the Atalanta story remained, at the end of the Artemis chapter, and Psyche's four tasks were incorporated into the Aphrodite chapter.

My interest in Atalanta was renewed the summer before I began writing this book, when I taught at the C. G. Jung Institute in Kusnacht, Switzerland for the first time. Kusnacht is Jung's hometown on the shore of Lake Zurich and, although I did not train there, I think of it as the "mothership" of Jungian institutes. For the first time in over a decade, I told the myth of Atalanta and amplified its meaning to an international student body. It came alive in me and in the room. I remembered why I had become interested in Atalanta in the first place.

Atalanta and Artemis

Atalanta is a famous hunter and runner in the ancient Greek myth of a mortal woman, who was rejected and left to die when she was born. She survived, the ancient storytellers said, because she was "under the protection of Artemis." Atalanta exemplifies the indomitable spirit in competent, courageous girls and in the women they become. This indomitable spirit refuses to give up on what she knows to be true for herself. These women have grit and the passion and persistence to go the distance, to survive and win.

Girls and women with indomitable spirit are the new protagonists in many of the most-read novels and fictional series of this century. They have emerged in the creative process of authors with a reality that seems to blend invention and active imagination. I believe that these emerging female heroes are captivating readers because of a morphic resonance. Energies and archetypal patterns in the collective unconscious are rising into our individual consciousness and changing assumptions about women and in women.

Katniss Everdeen is an Atalanta in Suzanne Collins' *The Hunger Games* trilogy; Lisbeth Salander is a darker side of this same spirit in Steig Larsson's *The Girl with the Dragon Tattoo.* I also see Atalanta in Anastasia Steele, the main character in E. L. James' *Fifty Shades of Grey* who ventured into the wilderness of emotion and sexuality. These are young women who call upon their intuition, depth of feeling, and courage to go beyond previous limits; who feel fear and outrage and have to adapt and endure and not give in or give up. Each has an inner spirit that is not subdued, a will that is not broken. Each in her own way is a quirky, independent, courageous person who is in uncharted territory—the metaphoric wilderness, the realm of Artemis.

Until the Women's Movement in the 1960s, the enduring fictional character with Atalanta qualities was independent-thinking, hot-tempered tomboy Jo from Louisa May Alcott's *Little Women.* Jo is the one sister in the March family who pursues a career and who, when she finally does marry, makes a conscious, personally meaningful choice. In novels, as in real life, it's not what happens to us that counts, but how we respond.

In Greek mythology, Atalanta the mortal and Artemis the goddess have similar sounding names and qualities. Artemis is the goddess with the silver bow and arrows, the hunter with unerring aim. Atalanta is also a renowned hunter. Like Artemis, she is at home in forests and associated with animals, the mother bear in particular. But Atalanta is mortal and, as such, can be affected by Artemis or any of the other divinities in the Greek pantheon. She can also suffer the consequences of being a woman in the cradle of patriarchy.

In the age of feminism, Atalanta became known to several generations of children through Marlo Thomas' *Free to Be . . . You and Me,* which entered the popular culture as a book, as a recording, and then as a television special. The book became a children's classic. In this version of the mythic tale, the Princess Atalanta is an athlete and astronomer who promises her father that she will marry the man who can beat her in a footrace. Atalanta has also been featured as a hunter and a runner in videogames, in comic books, and on television. She even became a toy action figure following her role as a strong character in the video series *Hercules: The Legendary Journeys.*

Goddess Archetypes in Everywoman

Goddesses in Everywoman introduced a new psychology of women based on archetypal patterns personified by eight major goddesses in classical mythology, one of whom was Artemis, archetype of the sister, competitor, goal achiever, and feminist. All archetypes are potentially active in every person—as lived out in us, projected onto others, or recognized when encountered in ancient myths or contemporary films. Just as we come into the world with innate natural gifts and personality traits that may be encouraged or suppressed depending upon expectations of family and society, so it is for the archetype of Artemis that Atalanta personifies.

The Artemis archetype was expressed at Seneca Falls in 1848, in the Declaration of Sentiments that was the beginning of the Women's Suffrage Movement, only one of which was the rallying issue of the right to vote. It took until 1920 for American women to gain this right through a constitutional amendment. Feminists in the mid-1960s through the 1970s emphasized sisterhood. They demanded equal access to education, jobs, and professions; they insisted on opportunities for girls to participate in sports; they demonstrated for reproductive rights. Thanks to their efforts, gains were made that rippled out into the world, but there was not enough support to pass the Equal Rights Amendment.

Even with the liberation of Artemis in American culture, there are some who hold to the same assumptions and values prevalent in cultures where a girl belongs to and obeys her father until she marries, after which she becomes her husband's possession. In these cultures, a woman's role is to maintain the household, please her husband, and bear male children. She must maintain her physical virginity before marriage, or at least the appearance of it. Sexuality is not for her own enjoyment, but for her husband's pleasure and the procreation of children. When virginity is the hallmark of value and honor, with bride price or dowry dependent upon it, women do not belong to themselves; they lack sovereignty and independence. When Hillary Clinton addressed the Fourth UN World Conference on Women in Beijing in 1995 with the ringing assertion that "Women's rights are human rights and human rights are women's rights," she brought attention to the reality that human rights are not extended to women—that democracy, even where it exists, often can only apply to men.

Artemis embodies the virgin-goddess archetype, a woman who is one-in-herself psychologically. She may or may not be a virgin physically; she may be of any age. The archetypal part of her maintains autonomy in her inner life, even when it is not allowed outward expression. She may need to keep her feelings, thoughts, and imagination of a different life to herself until she is old enough to leave a fundamentalist family headed by an authoritarian father. Or until she can join other women to express or protest, such as the women in India who demonstrated against authorities who disregard rape, those who joined One Billion Rising and danced in streets to end violence against women, or took part in the Arab Spring uprisings.

STORIES

In Jean M. Auel's *The Clan of the Cave Bear* (1980), Ayla is an orphaned five-year-old who is tolerated by people who are not like her own in prehistoric Europe. The way Ayla learns through observation and abuse, adapts and survives, and has her own goals is echoed by stories of real children and by women who see in Ayla something of themselves.

In *Game of Thrones*, Arya Stark is a young Artemis girl on her own in a devastated and dangerous world. Her once peaceful world was brought to an end, not by an earthquake which left Ayla orphaned, as natural disasters can do, but as a consequence of armed conflict. Wherever there are massive natural disasters and few resources, or ongoing fratricidal wars such as those in the Middle East and in central Africa now, and in Europe and Asia in the twentieth century, the psychological situation and dangers faced by these fictional girls are quite real to girls who lose parents, have no home to return to, and have the indomitable spirit and will to survive and not become helpless victims, no matter what. Anonymous to us, are the innumerable real life girls and women who are heroic and ordinary. Maybe you will recognize yourself as one.

The girl who does not give up on herself when others write her off as worthless taps into the indomitable spirit of Artemis, which is her archetype. This is the same source of indimitable will that is in the girl who devotes hours and years to master a skill or a sport or an art that takes commitment and practice. The bow and quiver of arrows which makes a sculpture or a painting of a goddess recognizable as Artemis is a meaningful symbol. To send an arrow to a target of your own choosing requires aim, intention, determination, focus and power. You can bring down game to feed yourself and others, punish enemies, or demonstrate confidence: metaphorically, you can take care of yourself.

When passion and perseverance come together day after day, the indomitable will that results can provide an energy to go beyond former limits. Diana Nyad is a stunning example of this. She was sixty-four when she became the first person to swim from Cuba to Florida in 2013, succeeding on her fifth attempt, the fourth since she turned sixty. She swam one hundred and three miles, took nearly fifty-three hours and did it in shark-infested water without a protective cage. Nyad said to Dr. Sanjay Gupta on CNN: "You have a dream that doesn't come to fruition, and move on with your life. But it is somewhere back there. And then you turn sixty, and your mom just dies, and you're looking for something. And the dream comes walking out of your imagination." While she was swimming, she got three messages: One is "never, ever give up," two is, "you are never too old to chase a dream," and the third was, "it looks like a solitary sport, but it's a team."

Stories are wonderful vehicles for images, feelings, atmosphere, and depth because they lead the readers or the audience to identify with and learn from the characters. We begin with our own experience and make a connection; something rings true and illuminates something important that we didn't recognize before about ourselves. When it reflects a deep truth, this insight is liberating. My hope for this book is that readers will find soul nourishment to grow into the people they were meant to be. By readers, I mean male as well as female readers. The ability to imagine ourselves as the main character, or even as all the characters, in a story, with no consideration as to the gender of that character makes us aware of the universality of the masculine and feminine in us all. This ability lets us recognize the qualities that are human and not gender-based.

When you *feel* personal and archetypal traits together, when there is a connection between you and the story that holds your attention, when you realize a truth that you have not before seen, this is an *aha!* moment—a moment when an unacknowleged archetype comes to life. For women in whom traditional roles and archetypes like daughter, wife, and mother (Persephone, Hera, and Demeter) coincide well with their expectations, Atalanta/Artemis may stay dormant until that moment of truth. Similarly, a woman who has been an Artemis and never wanted to be a mother, may, in her late thirties or early forties, feel that she must have a child if the maternal archetype lays a claim on her psyche.

The stories about Atalanta exemplify archetypal qualities of Artemis as goddess of the hunt. There is, as well, the meaning of Artemis as goddess of the moon, which is an affinity for mystical and meditative experiences, a sensing of subtle energies, a capacity for inner reflection. This lunar aspect is in activists who are "closet mystics," most recently attested to in Barbara Ehrenreich's *Living With a Wild God* (2014). Known for her books and essays about politics, economics, social class and women's issues, Ehrenreich wrote her unexpected memoir about mystical visions she had as a teenager, the extensive reading she has done since and the sense she makes of this personal reality as a scientist and atheist. Artemis is one of the three goddesses of the moon. She is the archetype of the waxing (or young and growing) crescent moon. Selene is the archetype of the full moon, while Hecate is the archetype of the waning crescent moon. In delving into these archetypes and their meanings, women can see and appreciate them as stages in themselves.

Artemis, Athena, and Hestia make up a second important trinity; they are the three Virgin Goddesses. As archetypes, they differ in attributes and values with one important quality in common: each has a one-in-herself inner core. Intelligent strategy is Athena's gift, introverted centeredness is Hestia's.

Atalanta and Artemis are the means through which readers can drop into their own depth psychology. There are many real-life stories of women in these pages, as well as mythological and fictional examples of women who are similar to Atalanta. If Artemis is a strong archetype in your psyche, you will see reflections of yourself and will value the indomitable qualities that have sustained you. You may also realize how you may need to grow. It may also be that you are someone who has imagined yourself in the stories about indomitable girls and women, but has kept this part of yourself under wraps. If so, perhaps this book—or a vivid dream, or synchronicity—may help you to realize that an indomitable spirit exists in you. And, with right timing and courage, you will be true to the Artemis in yourself.

Chapter One

ATALANTA THE MYTH

Stories often change with the telling and the point of view of the storyteller. In Greek mythology, there were two versions of Atalanta's origins as a famous hunter from either Arcadia (as told by Apollodorus) or Boetia (as told by Hesiod). In Ovid's *Metamorphoses*, Greek myths were assembled and retold in Latin verse. I describe Atalanta as being from Arcadia because it is in this version that we get the account of her birth and how she was abandoned and suckled by a bear.

Atalanta is also mentioned as wanting to enlist with Jason and the Argonauts on their search for the Golden Fleece. She is refused because her presence as a woman among men would be disruptive—the same argument that was used to keep women from serving in the military until recently. This didn't stop Atalanta, however, as told by classical scholar Robert Graves (*The Golden Fleece*, 1944). Graves describes how, as the Argo casts off, Atalanta jumps aboard and, invoking the protection of Artemis (for her virginity), joins the heroes. In another vignette, when two centaurs try to rape her, she kills them with her arrows.

I have taken liberties as a storyteller to combine elements from separate myths in which Atalanta is mentioned, adding some embellishments. For example, when I tell how the bear finds her, I incorporate Bernard Evslin's version of how she and Meleager meet (*Heroes, Gods, and Monsters of the Greek Myths*, 1968). I tell of her return to Arcadia after the hunt for the boar to provide continuity between the hunt and the footrace. Here is the story as I tell it.

THE MYTH OF ATALANTA

In the kingdom of Arcadia, the king is eagerly awaiting the birth of his first-born. When the new baby proves not to be the son and heir he expects, he vents his anger on his unwanted daughter and orders a shepherd to take her to a nearby mountain and leave her there to die of exposure or an attack by a wild animal. Atalanta begins her life unwanted and rejected. But what was intended as the end of her life in fact turns out to be an unusual beginning.

The shepherd does as he is told. He takes the baby and places her among the rocks on the mountain. Atalanta wails; she is hungry, wet, and cold. Her cries attract a mother bear whose den is somewhere nearby. Whether out of curiosity or maternal instinct, the bear investigates and sniffs the baby. Atalanta grasps the fur of the bear and the human infant and mother bear bond. The mother bear takes the baby to her den, suckles her, and keeeps her warm. It was said that the goddess Artemis sent the bear.

Bear cubs are small and helpless when they are born. Like human babies, they cannot survive without maternal care. They grow to adulthood faster than human babies, however, so Atalanta is raised with a succession of cubs as siblings. In another version of the tale, when she is able to walk, she is found by hunters who raise her and teach her to hunt and speak.

Meleager

At about the same time that Atalanta is born, in the neighboring kingdom of Calydon, another king eagerly awaits the birth of his first-born. It is a boy! The son is named Meleager and his birth is greeted with festivities and celebration.

Shortly after Meleager is born, an unusual visitor—Atropos, one of the three Fates—calls upon Meleager's mother. A blazing fire heats the room in which the queen receives her guest. Atropos goes to the fireplace, stands on the hearth, and points to a log that is burning on one end. She says: "Do you see this? As long as it remains unconsumed, your son will live!" The queen leaps up, grasps the log, and smothers the flames. She then wraps it up, locks it in a brass chest, and hides the chest and the secret away. Meleager's life (or death) has been put into his mother's hands.

Meleager grows to manhood, raised to someday become king. Tutors teach him what he is expected to know to fill this role. His mother concentrates on finding him a suitable wife. Meleager spends as little time as he can in the castle. He prefers to be in the forests and wilderness of Calydon. Every so often, his mother insists that he meet an eligible young woman from a suitable family. Time and time again, the matchmaking fails. Meleager isn't interested in soft, frilly, feminine, simpering girls with whom he has nothing in common. "Find me a girl," he says, "who can join me in the outdoors, who can be my companion."

Atalanta and Meleager

One day when Meleager is out hunting, he hears the sound of a large animal and sees that it is a bear—a worthy trophy for him. With his strong arm and bow, he sends an arrow into the bear, wounding it badly, but not fatally. The bear, in pain and loosing blood, instinctively goes in the direction of its den, away from Calydon. Meleager follows, intent on bringing the bear down. The bear plunges through the brush and trees, hour after hour, mile after mile, losing blood and getting weaker as the day goes on. Finally, at the foothill of a mountain, the bear collapses.

Meleager has just caught up with the bear, when he sees a woman coming down the mountain toward him. He is immediately enthralled. She is everything that the girls he knows at court are not. She is as beautiful as any creature in nature—sun-tanned, long-haired, long-limbed, graceful, athletic—his dream girl!

"I am Meleager," he tells her. "I killed this bear, and I will give his pelt to you as a trophy!"

"I am Atalanta," she replies. "That bear is my brother, and now I will kill you!"

Atalanta rushes at him with killing on her mind. But Meleager, now smitten, has love on his. They are evenly matched and it seems as if they wrestle for hours.

Outdoors in the mountain air, with the smell of crushed grasses under them, both perspire as they wrestle, skin to skin. Atalanta's focus shifts to being in this totally new experience. This is the first time she has wrestled with a human being like herself—the first time she has felt skin rather than fur. The embrace begins with her wanting to kill Meleager, and him holding her to prevent it. As they struggle in this embrace, however, new feelings and curiosity arise in her.

However it happens, Meleager and Atalanta become a couple. Soon they become famous. Seen hunting together, they are a handsome pair, each as striking as the other in appearance and in skill. Meleager's mother seethes when she learns about the relationship. Atalanta is totally inappropriate for her son! She is truly a nobody, a rustic with no known family, and totally without social graces. Definitely not a proper young woman to become queen someday.

Meanwhile, the king has a major problem on his hands—a huge boar sent to devastate his kingdom by an outraged goddesss. He brought this on his kingdom by neglecting to honor Artemis in the yearly rites. Meleager's new girlfriend is probably not as much of a concern to him as the destruction caused by this creature.

The Hunt for the Calydon Boar

The boar is enormous. With its sharp curved tusks and its huge feet, it rages through fields, destroying crops and trampling domesticated animals and people who can not get out of its way. It destroys villages and threatens the whole countryside. Artemis, Goddess of the Hunt, fashioned the boar out of mud and gave it life in retaliation against the king who neglected her while making sacrifices to other divinities. Although this is the usual reason given for her wrath, however, another cause may be the awe that people feel toward Atalanta, a mere human. When they look at Atalanta as if she were Artemis, this offends the goddess.

Regardless of the cause, the boar has to be dealt with. The king invites the heroes of Greece to gain honor and reward for themselves by hunting it. Among those who answer the challenge are many of the heroes who went with Jason as Argonauts and later took part in the Trojan War.

The heroes assemble prior to the hunt. The last to arrive are Meleager and Atalanta. The other hunters are scandalized. Even though she is now a famous hunter, how dare a woman join the hunt! There is muttering among the men, with Meleager's uncles speaking aloud against having Atalanta there, using demeaning words. Meleager rises to her defense, draws his sword, and challenges them. Cooler heads prevail and all are reminded that they are, after all, there to kill the boar.

It is a large hunting party of very strong, wily men, each wanting fame and reward for taking down the boar. Some are slashed or gored or trampled in the attempt. The canny boar takes its stand in a place where hunters can not act as a group, but have to attack the boar singly or in pairs. None of them succeed in even wounding the animal, because the boar's pelt is impervious to arrows and spears.

No one draws blood, until Atalanta faces the boar. The boar charges straight at her, its razor-sharp tusks now covered with blood, its massive weight bearing down upon her. Atalanta's bowstring is taut, her arrow at the ready, her eye steady. The boar is almost to her when, with unerring aim, she sends an arrow through one of its eyes, penetrating its brain. It staggers, but is not dead. Now it is Meleager's turn to act. He takes his sword and delivers the death blow.

The boar is dead! Meleager has the right to the pelt, but, instead of claiming it for himself, he gives it to Atalanta. This is truly an important trophy and there is resentment among the others that a woman should have it. It isn't just that it is a symbol of a major heroic achievement that will bring fame to the one who possesses it. This pelt can be made into a garment that is flexible, warm, and impervious to spear and arrow. There could be no better armor.

Meleager's uncles are enraged. Such a prize should not go to a woman! If Meleager doesn't want it for himself, then, they—as his male relatives—should have it and not Atalanta! They speak against her. One of them attempts to snatch the pelt from her. Meleager responds with his drawn sword, lopping off first this uncle's head and then the other's; silencing all protest.

Now it is time to return to the castle with news of the death of the boar. All but Atalanta and Meleager tramp back to the castle, where the king and queen await them. The returning hunters come back with good news—the boar is dead. And then comes the bad news—Meleager has killed his uncles, the queen's brothers.

The queen now learns that Atalanta shot the arrow that drew first blood and Meleager then killed the boar and gave the trophy to her. Then she learns how Meleager was provoked by his uncles' insulting words and their disrespect to Atalanta, and how he killed them. This is too much for her. Maddened by this news, the queen goes to where she hid the locked chest. She opens it and takes out the log given to her by Atropos. Then she orders the servants to build a fire—and throws the log in.

The Death of Meleager

Atalanta and Meleager do not return to the castle after the hunt. They stay with each other where they are most at home, in the wilderness of the forest and hills. They are in each other's arms when, suddenly, Meleager makes a horrible sound and, clutching his abdomen, cries out in pain. Then his torso blackens as if burned, his face turns ashen, and he dies.

Atalanta grieves for him. Nature is her only solace. She weeps and wanders for weeks in the forest and glades. Then, one day, she realizes that she must leave this place that reminds her of Meleager and their time together. With him gone, there is nothing here to hold her and no one who matters.

And so, she leaves Calydon and travels through forests and over hills toward Arcadia.

THE FOOTRACE AND THE GOLDEN APPLES

Meanwhile, the fame of Atalanta has traveled to the neighboring kingdom. The heroes who return from the Calydon hunt tell about her beauty and prowess as a hunter. When Atalanta arrives home, her description and fame have preceded her. The king welcomes her and, perhaps from her story or appearance, realizes that she is the daughter that he ordered exposed on the mountain years before. In the intervening years, he has not had a son and heir. Now he recognizes Atalanta as his daughter—a daughter more accomplished and famous than any son he might have had.

Atalanta is now not only beautiful and famous; but she is also an heiress to a kingdom. This makes her very marriageable. After many suitors turn up, her father demands that she must marry one of them for the sake of the kingdom.

Atalanta doesn't want to marry anyone. When her father insists, she finally agrees, but only under one condition. The man she marries must be able to beat her in a footrace. And if he loses the race, he must forfeit his life.

Many men, thinking they can beat her, accept this challenge. But Atalanta is swift and wins race after race. Men come from afar, lose to her, and forfeit their lives.

Finally, only one man remains to race her—Hippomenes, a most unlikely suitor. All of the other men who accepted the challenge thought that by beating Atalanta they would acquire a kingdom and a famous and beautiful wife. Hippomenes, on the other hand, knows he can not win the race. He is not a heroic figure; he is not particularly strong or swift as a runner. Nonetheless, he intends to enter the race. He has followed Atalanta from Calydon. He knows of her love for and loss of Meleager and has compassion for what happened. In short, he loves her.

On the evening before the race, Hippomenes prays to Aphrodite, Goddess of Love and Beauty. He prays that Atalanta may love him and for there to be a way for him to win her. All the others who had lost the race (and their lives) had prayed to other gods to be able to overcome and possess her. Some prayed to Hermes for speed, others to Zeus to overpower her, others to Ares for strength to beat her.

Aphrodite hears Hippomenes' prayers and appears to him with three golden apples and some advice. On awakening, he thinks it was all a dream—until he sees the three apples.

The next morning, Atalanta stands at the starting line waiting for Hippomenes to arrive. She has noticed him before, and wished that he would not race her, since the outcome is inevitable. He is no match for her as a runner.

Hippomenes arrives clutching his arms around his waistband, holding the three golden apples out of sight. This strikes Atalanta as peculiar, and then it reminds her of how Meleager clutched his abdomen just before he died in her arms. She goes into a reverie, taking her mind off the race. So when the signal to start is given, Hippomenes runs as fast as he can, but Atalanta is not prepared. Startled by the realization that the race has begun, she runs to catch up. As she draws even with Hippomenes, he drops a golden apple. The rolling motion of the apple catches her eye and reminds her of how the heads had rolled when Meleager came to her defense.

The apple is irresistible. Its golden glow and beauty draw her and she has to stop to pick it up. She gazes at it and sees a reflection of her own face, distorted by the curves of the apple.

Meanwhile, Hippomenes races ahead. Atalanta is so swift, however, that she soon overtakes him once again. Then he drops the second apple, which rolls across her path and to the side. Again she stops to pick it up.

Now Hippomenes is in the lead, with the finish line in view. Atalanta puts on a spurt of speed and catches up with him. At this moment, Hippomenes drops the third apple. If she ignores it, she will win the race. If she picks it up, she will lose the race. Atalanta reaches for the apple as Hippomenes crosses the finish line. He wins the race and Atalanta in marriage. But did she let him win?

The Meaning of the Myth

The end of the footrace is not the end of the personal story for women who resemble Atalanta. It is, more likely, the beginning of the second half of their lives. This is also not the end of Atalanta's mythic story. There are versions of the myth that do not end with the race, but go on to tell how Atalanta and Hippomenes are punished and transformed into a pair of lions and yoked together to pull a divine chariot. The story deepens when these events are seen as metaphors and interpreted as symbolic.

While Atalanta is a mortal in the image of Artemis, her life is influenced and changed by more than one goddess. Through Hippomenes, Atalanta feels the spell of Aphrodite's golden apples. This is the case with contemporary women as well. All of the goddesses are potential archetypal patterns in every woman and, while Artemis may be dominant in the first third of a woman's life and can remain a strong influence, often one or more other archetypes may emerge in the second and third phases of life.

Atalanta's story has the power of a big dream with many layers of meaning. At first, it is intriguing to take in the whole story with the images that come to mind as you read it. Even at first glance, a particular image or detail may catch your imagination. Enduring myths are similar to important dreams that people remember because there is "something" to them. They touch the psyche of the dreamer, reader, or listener, even without interpretation. Atalanta is a mortal and is like a real woman who appears in a dream or in life, bringing the archetype of Artemis or a quality of Artemis to life. When this happens, a woman who is like Atalanta can become a combination of goddess and mortal to others.

The story of Atalanta becomes very personal to girls and women who find similarities between her qualities and their own—between her story and theirs. It can also give some insight into often difficult and painful experiences for men and women who love or have loved them. Being in a relationship with a woman like Atalanta whose dominant archetype is Artemis can be more difficult or challenging to others than being her. A prime example: Nobel Laureate poet William Butler Yeats, whose yearning love for beautiful, fiery, feminist Irish revolutionary Maud Gonne was immortalized in his verse across five decades. She married someone else, and much later, he did also.

Delving into a myth is very much like working with a dream. To understand the meaning or interpretation, a Jungian analyst works with the person whose dream it is, amplifying elements in it, which is what I will be doing with the myth of Atalanta in this book. Myths have the power of collective dreams and fascinate us because the themes in them are ours to inhabit or to observe.

Chapter Two

ATALANTA, ARTEMIS, MOTHER BEAR

Mother bears are ferociously protective and extraordinarily nurturing. Good advice to people headed into the wilderness is *never* to get between a mother bear and her cubs! Mother bears have qualities that make them really good mothers. They are notably fierce in defense of their young; they are also good caretakers. Bear cubs are born in the winter months—usually in January and February, while the mother bear is in hibernation. Newborn bears are smaller than newborn human babies, weighing around ten ounces at birth. They can't open their eyes and are kept warm in their mother's fur and by her breath. They suckle instinctively and grow rapidly on the fat-rich milk, emerging only in early spring when they are big enough and strong enough to walk, run, and explore.

A mother bear sleeps only when her babies sleep. Initially, the cubs nurse every ten minutes. They are noisy, make humming noises when awake and suckling, and cry when they need something. The mother bear washes them often with her tongue, and puts them on a teat when they can't find one. Once the cubs leave the den, the mother will continue to suckle them until they are weaned. She then teaches them what berries they can eat, how to catch fish, and how to hunt. The cubs learn to climb trees for safety when there may be danger on the ground. They have little to fear when they are in their mother's sight—the biggest exception being the dangers posed by bad actors of their own species. Predatory male bears eat cubs.

When the cubs are able to take care of themselves, the mother bear makes them independent of her. She sends them up a tree, just as when she was teaching them to climb to safety, only this last time, she doesn't come back for them. They are old enough to be self-sufficient; now they must climb down and fend for themselves.

I am reminded here of a woman who described how she took animal mothers as role models for herself. On becoming pregnant, fearful that her own mother's unmaternal example may have rubbed off on her, she did the opposite and turned to the example of animal mothers—and particularly mother bears. I might add here that her own mother's behavior may have been caused by male "experts" on child-rearing who told young mothers to put babies on feeding schedules, to toilet train them early, and not to spoil them by giving in to their crying. This was also a time when it seemed that only foreigners and the poor nursed their children; middle- and upper-class women did not.

According to these "experts," to be a competent modern mother was a matter of having a stronger will than the baby's. To comfort a fussy baby or to nurse on demand was frowned upon. This deprived both mother and child. The effect on young mothers was to suppress their bodies (drying up the milk) and to suppress the maternal instinct to respond to a crying baby. By doing what they were told, young mothers missed learning that they could instinctively distinguish levels of distress in their children, and could help and be comforting. Instead, a whole generation of American mothers got further lessons in hierarchy: Do what others tell you to do; believe what others say rather than what you feel yourself.

The pendulum eventually swung away from the "show the child who is boss" school of parenting to more permissive parenting, in which nothing must diminish the self-esteem of the child. In this version, a good mother and an indulgent one tended to become one and the same. While you can't spoil an *infant* by always responding to its distress or by providing whatever it needs, doing so long after infancy does spoil character. Shielding children from disappointments, not teaching them limits and limitations, and excessively praising them for every little thing prolongs childhood and isn't good preparation for responsible adolescence or adulthood. Time to call upon mother bear as a role model!

Mother Bear—Symbol of Artemis

The bear is a symbol of the protective aspect of Artemis. Artemis is particularly protective of girls and women. She is characterized as a virgin goddess and never as a mother. Yet she is the goddess to whom young pre-pubescent girls were dedicated; they were then referred to as the *arktoi* or "little bears." During the year that young girls were sanctified under Artemis' protection, they were safe from early marriage and had the freedom from women's constrictions in dress and behavior. They could play as boys did and were free to be outdoors—very much like nine- to twelve-year-old "tomboys."

I look back on summers at Girl Scout Camp and realize that these were a*rtktoi* experiences for me. The camp drew children from the Los Angeles area, busing us up to Big Bear Lake—to terrain dear to the goddess Artemis—where there were meadows, forests, mountains, lakes, and streams. We learned how to make campfires, use a compass, tie knots, carve with a knife, and recognize star constellations, trees, and various flora and fauna. We hiked a lot, sang together around the campfire and while hiking, slept under the stars, showered sometimes, wore wrinkled nondescript clothes (except for the "greenie tops" that had a somewhat uniform look), and stowed our stuff away in a shared tent in case of rain. We were from many parts of the city and surrounding areas. At camp, we did not have to live up to any image we had at school; we didn't spend time concerned about our reflections in mirrors or in how boys saw us. We learned about ourselves and each other, and shared confidences. While our parents sent us away to camp the first time, we returned there by choice. It was meaningful and fun because we had the Artemis archetype in common—the archetype of sister. When this is an active archetype in a girl or woman, she has a sense of sisterhood and an affinity to feminist causes.

Artemis is twin sister to Apollo. While Apollo is God of the Sun, with his golden bow and arrows, Artemis is Goddess of the Moon, with her bow and arrows of silver. She is also called Artemis *Eileithyria* and is the goddess of childbirth and the divine midwife, because she helped her mother, Leto, through the longest and most difficult labor in mythology. Leto was impregnated by Zeus, the chief god in Greek mythology, and bore the twins, Artemis and Apollo. Because Zeus' wife, Hera, was angered by the pregnancy, no one dared offer Leto shelter or aid.

Artemis is born first. After her delivery, Hera causes Leto to suffer and go into prolonged labor. But divinities are not like mortals, and newborn Artemis becomes her mother's midwife, helping to deliver Apollo. Consequently, in ancient Greece, women prayed to Artemis for swift delivery from the pain of childbirth. Contemporary midwives and women who choose obstetrics and gynecology as medical specialties to help women and reduce their fear and pain in childbirth are thus being true to this aspect of Artemis.

Artemis is the only goddess who often came to the rescue of women in other circumstances. She saves Arethusa from being raped; she protects or avenges her mother's honor when a giant tries to rape her and when a mortal woman demeans her. In these stories, Artemis is fierce in her protectiveness, like a mother bear. Or like activists who rescue trafficked girls from brothels and provide gynecological and psychological care to rape victims. Or like those who lead demonstrations to seek justice for raped girls and women in India, or lobby the United States Congress to pass the Violence Against Women Act, or advocate for a United Nations World Conference on Women. Or like anyone, in fact, who works toward equality for women and the protection of mothers and children.

Mother-Bear Support

Girls raised metaphorically by mother bear can be children nurtured by Mother Nature. They may be drawn to animals and find solace outdoors. They may feel safer and more at home under a tree or currying horses in a stable than in a home where they may be neglected or abused. When these girls find mother bear in themselves and find the support to be themselves in the archetype symbolized by the protective mother bear, they become competitors in the world. It is the archetype of Artemis that comes to the aid of these girls who, in some significant way, were abandoned and then found in nature or with animals the parents that they did not have at home. It may also be their nature as an Artemis to prefer to be in the woods, uninterested in staying at home or in doing womanly or girlish things.

I have known many women in my psychiatric and analytic practice and in my life who, like Atalanta, were psychologically abandoned and then raised by "mother bear." As girls, they came from families where parental figures neglected, rejected, or abused them emotionally or physically, or where parents, because of illness, death, or circumstance, could not be fully present. As a result, at a psychological and spiritual level, they had to raise themselves. They also instinctively kept up appearances, worked at making good grades or excelling at sports, and acted as if their home lives were normal. It is natural for their Artemis nature to follow examples we see in nature. Nature provides animals with protective coloration so they don't stand out. When animals are wounded or weakened, they know to hide their vulnerability to avoid becoming prey.

Gloria Steinem wrote of herself: "I remembered feeling sad about navigating life by myself, working after school, worrying about my mother, who was sometimes too removed from reality to know where she was, or who I was, and concealing these shameful family secrets from my friends . . . now as then, I turn away sympathy with jokes and a survivor's pride" (*Revolution From Within*, 1992). Artemis is the archetype that protects the young girl who instinctively hides her vulnerability during the years of middle school and high school.

Girls who are not under the protection of Artemis may reveal rather than hide vulnerability, which can mark them as potential victims to be preyed on, bullied, or made scapegoats. Recent media attention focused on two young girls, ages fifteen and seventeen, who hanged themselves. It's an old story: Girl has too much to drink at a party and passes out; boys take turns having sex with her; her name is passed around at school; then other boys want her to "put out" for them, too. She becomes known as a "slut" and is shunned by the "good" girls. A new variation on the theme makes it worse: While one of the young men is fucking her (what else can it be called?), there are "clicks" as another or others use their smartphones to take photos or videos that are posted online and circulated around the school. Eventually, and in despair, the two young girls killed themselves.

I mentioned hearing about these two teenage suicides at the Pacifica Writers Conference in Santa Barbara and learned from Donna DeNomme (*Ophelia's Oracle*, 2009) about an "Artemis girl" who did not accept being a victim and whose story had a very different ending. What she told me warmed my heart and was the best kind of encouragement, since, at the time, I was writing *Artemis* with the intention that it would help women to see themselves in this myth—younger women especially.

Donna described the situation in an email to me:

One less-than-popular girl was thrilled to be included by her girlfriend with an invitation to attend a party.

At that party her delight turned to terror as she was raped. Her so-called girlfriend filmed the violation and uploaded the video to the Internet. When the victim arrived at school on Monday, she was taunted by classmates for what they may have thought was consensual sex. The traumatized girl, who had been given Ophelia's Oracle *by her grandmother a few months before, said it was the story about the boldness of Artemis in the book that gave her the courage to press charges against the boy who raped her, the girl who filmed the rape, and the mother of one of the teens who bought beer for the kids and then left them alone in her house. She told her grandmother: "Artemis would want me to do this."*

When I wrote *Goddesses in Everywoman*, I provided exemplars of each of the goddess archetypes that were public figures. Gloria Steinem, as a founder of *Ms.* magazine and a beautiful spokesperson for feminism, was a natural choice for Artemis. Her concerns for girls and women, her competency and courage to stand for and stand up for equality and empowerment of women, are clearly those of the archetype. However, Gloria—like all women—is more than an embodiment of one archetype. While one archetype may be the strongest, all of the others are potential sources of meaning in every woman. And not every facet of the strongest archetype has to be lived out or felt in each woman. Gloria is like a mother bear in her protectiveness and in responding to appeals for help from women, but she is hardly noted for being a woman in the wilderness.

Julia Butterfly Hill, on the other hand, spent two years living in an ancient redwood tree exposed to the elements in order to prevent the logging of an old-growth forest in Northern California. She is a symbol of an environmental activist who embodies this aspect of the archetype.

While an activist becomes proactive in response to or in protest against something happening in the outer world, the goddess-of-the-moon aspect of the Atalanta archetype explains the capacity for reflection—to draw back from activity, to think about motivation and meaning, to see by moonlight or reflected light. In the wilderness, moonlight illuminates; there is beauty and mystery—a oneness I experienced as a Girl Scout in the wilderness that became the source of later understanding that I drew on in writing *The Tao of Psychology* (1999). Sleeping outdoors under the nighttime sky with the Milky Way overhead, paying close attention so that I might see a shooting star (probably a comet) to make a wish on—these experiences prepared the way for me to slip into an altered state of consciousness. They prepared me to recognize that I was part of everything out there. They brought me an inner certainty, even before I had words for or knew of the concept of oneness that underlies all visible manifestations. It was mystical insight, and so very Artemis.

To be able to take to the woods, to turn to animals or to books, to have a rich imagination, or to be nourished by solitude are solitary activities that feed self-sufficiency—a quality needed and strengthened in girls who have to raise themselves because of inadequate, absent, disabled, or abusive parents. Artemis can be alive in the inner lives of girls and women when there is no room for autonomy, education, or protest in the world they live in. In the inner world of the imagination, a girl can be heroic; she can have a place in her psyche that identifies with global expressions of feminism that are condemned or ridiculed. She has an archetypal connection with Artemis, even if she must remain obedient or subservient, and is forced to marry young. I suspect that this accounts for the women who demonstrated during the Arab Spring against dictatorship, surprising the world with the fact that they even existed.

The Will to Live and Help to Survive

In my years of medical training, as I observed newborn babies in the nursery, I realized that personality traits show up early. Some newborns are quiet and placid when they are picked up from the bassinette; others protest loudly when disturbed. Most seem to spend their time asleep, but others look around and stay awake more. There are fussy babies who cry a lot and others who rarely do. Levels of passivity and activity differ.

I was taught as a resident in psychiatry that babies are like a *tabula raza* (blank tablet) on which experience writes character and personality. This theory puts mothers at fault for everything, including sexual orientation and psychiatric illnesses. While pediatrician and psychoanalyst Donald W. Winnicott's concept of the "good-enough mother" (*Winnicott Studies*, 1994) helped mitigate the impact of this theory and lessened the pressure on mothers, mothers were still held to be the responsible ones; fathers were neither praised nor blamed. The unique personality of the baby itself was hardly ever mentioned, much less emphasized. It took having two babies of my own to learn what mothers have known all along—that, far from being a blank slate upon which we write, babies come with predispositions and train their mothers. They push buttons in their mothers' psyches and draw out aspects and responses—for better or worse.

I also suspect that infant girls and toddlers who survive illnesses that were expected to kill them—or were abandoned shortly after birth and then are found alive, or who survived terrible physical assaults—have an inherent or archetypal will to live. They draw upon an indomitable spirit, a characteristic of Artemis that shows up early when it has to. One amazing true story of survival, found in *The Girl with No Name* (Chapman, et.al., 2013), tells of a five-year-old toddler who was probably kidnapped and then abandoned in the Colombian jungle. The child stayed on the periphery of a troop of Capuchin monkeys, eating what they ate. She was taken in by the monkeys and grew up feral and walking on all fours until she was found and maltreated by humans, which began another whole saga of survival. The child's birth name was never discovered; she now goes by the name Marina Chapman. Marina made me wonder if Atalanta could have been a real person about whom stories were told—a little girl who became a mythical figure, a girl thought to have been suckled by a bear and found by hunters.

PATRIARCHAL POWER

Greek mythology, like Greek society, was patriarchal. Male gods were powerful and territorial. Their use of power to dominate or rule over others was taken for granted, and men made in their image assumed the same rights. In classical Greek mythology, rape was a common theme. Zeus, the chief god of Olympus, tricked, seduced, raped, impregnated, and abandoned the mothers of his many progeny.

Patriarchal systems are always hierarchal, symbolized as a pyramid or mountain, with the most desirable position at the top. Humans, animals, plants, the ocean, and minerals are all exploited and used for the profit and power of those at the top of the mountain. Conflicts and wars are fought over who will occupy the top of the pyramid, with destruction of life, beauty, and hope found in every war zone. Rape is used as a metaphor when applied to cities and to the earth itself; but wherever there is war, women are raped. Today, in the Congo, rape is deliberately used as a means of conducting war. Eve Ensler, returning from the Congo, refers to patriarchy as a "Rape Culture" (*In the Body of the World*, 2013). This made me think about how Zeus on Mount Olympus, the symbolic progenitor of patriarchy, was a serial rapist.

From archeological evidence, most notably that described by UCLA archeologist Marija Gimbutas (*The Goddesses and Gods of Old Europe*, 1982), we know that. Europe's first civilization, from 6,500 to 5,000 BCE, was matrifocal, sedentary, and peaceful. Its members created art and worshipped goddesses. Successive waves of invaders from the distant north and east, referred to as Indo-Europeans or Kurgans, conquered these earlier peoples. The invaders were nomadic, horse-riding, warlike tribes who worshipped sky gods. They regarded themselves as superior to the peaceful and more culturally developed people of Old Europe, whom they easily subjugated. Male gods and male superiority came to be assumed as the natural order. In the historical time when Athens became known as the "cradle of democracy," the right of citizenship was given only to men. Fathers had the power of life or death over their newborn children, which meant that an unwanted daughter or a defective infant could be disposed of, and a daughter who lost her virginity could be sold into slavery.

Not much has changed in some parts of the world. There are still places where a young daughter can be sold into marriage to a much older man who may already have several wives. The prospective husband and her father merely agree upon a dowry or bride price. Or a daughter may be sold for an agreed price to a human trafficker who takes her to a brothel. Her virginity must be assured in both instances, as her value depends upon it. Under this code, since a virgin who is raped dishonors the men of her family, a brother, a father, an uncle, or a grandfather has the right to murder her. This awful practice is called "honor killing." Mothers have no say in the fate of their daughters or, for that matter, in their own fate, since their primary function is to be brood mares. How very different if, instead, these women were mother bears!

In "Sarah Palin, Mama Grizzlies, Carl Jung, and the Power of Archetypes," Arianna Huffington looked to "that under-appreciated political pundit, Carl Jung" to explain Sarah Palin's appeal (*Huffington Post*, August 1, 2010). She cites "Mama Grizzlies," Palin's web video compiled from a series of Palin rallies, with sound-bite responses.

> *"It seems like it's kind of a mom awakening . . . women are rising up."*

"I always think of the mama grizzly bears that rise up on their hind legs when somebody is coming to attack their cubs."

Huffington notes that it is not Palin's political positions that people respond to; it's her use of symbols.

Mama grizzles rearing up to protect their young? That's straight out of Jung's "collective unconscious"—the term Jung used to describe the part of the unconscious mind that, unlike the personal unconscious, is shared by all human beings, made up of archetypes, or, in Jung's words, "universal images that have existed since the remotest times."

When women in India take to the streets to protest official disregard of rape, when women dance in the streets in an outpouring of support for Eve Ensler's One Billion Rising demonstrations to stop violence against women and girls, when the number of nongovernmental organizations (NGOs) working toward empowerment and equality for women and girls grows exponentially, women across the world are rising up, led by feminists for whom Artemis and mother-bear activism are deep sources of meaning, even when these forces are not named. When they are, there is an immediate "aha!" of intuitive recognition, becauseecause these are archetypal energies that are found in many cultures.

GENDERCIDE

When Atalanta is born, her father expresses his anger and his rejection in a horrible way. Today, the birth of a girl can still be a cause of disappointment, resentment, or anger. In China, for instance, under the "one child per family" policy, girl babies may literally be abandoned in railroad stations and other public places where they will be found and taken to a state-run orphanage. In rural areas, where infanticide is more common, newborn girls may be drowned, smothered, or starved, the family claiming that they died "in childbirth" or shortly after. The same is true in parts of India.

In a 2011 newspaper article, "Girls Choose Better Names" (*San Francisco Chronicle*, October 23), Chaya Babu reported from Mumbai that 285 girls shed names like Nakusa or Nakushi, which mean "unwanted" in Hindi, and chose new names for a fresh start in life. The plight of girls in India came into focus as this year's census showed the nation's ratio for children under the age of six had dropped to 914 girls for every 1,000 boys. Such ratios indicate a higher death rate among girls due to abortion of female fetuses, female infanticide, or neglect of female children.

Normally between 103 and 106 boys are born for every 100 girls. The ratio has been stable enough to indicate a natural order across races and cultures, one that resulted in approximately the same number of young men and young women, taking into account that, genetically, males are slightly more vulnerable and slightly more likely to die in infancy than girls. The change in this natural order was dramatically illustrated on the cover of *The Economist* (March 6–12, 2010), which carried the word "Gendercide" printed in bright pink on a black background. Under this startling headline was the question: "What Happened to 100 Million Baby Girls?" The serious article within concluded that these girls had either been killed, aborted, or neglected to the point that they died. When girl babies are not valued and prenatal sex-determination is linked with declining fertility as well as the selective abortion of female fetuses, a disproportionate number of male children survive, skewing the ratio of boys to girls. According to the Chinese Academy of Social Sciences, by 2020 there will be thirty to forty million more young men than young women in China because of the preference for boys. In India in 2001, there were forty-six districts with a sex ratio of over 125 boys to 100 girls.

It is not just a skewed birth rate that is reflected in there being fewer females in the world. There are also fewer girls and fewer women surviving than can be expected. Girls don't get the same healthcare and food as boys in impoverished countries. In India, girls from one to five years of age are 50 percent more likely to die from preventable causes than boys their age. Women die unnecessarily in childbirth due to inadequate medical care, or due to lack of contraception and choice. Pregnancy carries greater risks when the mother is very young or weakened by multiple pregnancies and poor nutrition. Then there are deaths of women from the collateral damage of armed conflict, especially when rape is used as a weapon, which is the case in many parts of Africa. And rape becomes an even more common and horrifying gender hazard when accompanied by mutilation and severe beatings, as it is in families and communities where the victim is blamed and may be turned out to live on the streets.

Experts have revised upward the estimate of missing girls from 100 million to 160 million. Jeni Klugman, Director of Gender and Development for the World Bank, called this "femicide" in a talk at the United Nations that drew from the World Development Report for 2012. According to this report, four million women go missing annually. These are obviously conclusions drawn from inadequate information, in the realm of what laymen call "guesstimates," or "educated guesses." But questioning numbers like these or doubting their accuracy sometimes allows us to ignore their human impact. When we turn people into inanimate statistics, we numb our emotional reaction to them. When we try to wrap our minds around such appalling numbers, we lose sight of their real meaning. One remedy is to think in smaller numbers. What if it were only a "mere" million, or only 100,000, or just 10,000? What if it were your daughter or yourself or your very young grandchild? It is important to be able to imagine being helpless, to imagine the horror of being abducted, beaten, and raped, or of being sold or turned by fear and pain into prostitution, as occurs in human trafficking.

When I go to panels and presentations that are given by UN NGOs (nongovernmental organizations recognized by the United Nations) or by the UN Commission on the Status of Women, they usually focus on women and girls during the meetings. At these events, women from every continent come together to address women's issues. Many of these organizations were founded by women who themselves had been victimized, but did not take on the role of victim. For others, this work feels like a vocation—a calling to help women who suffer in a number of ways, among them human trafficking, AIDS, or female genital mutilation (FMG). This barbaric, religiously sanctioned practice of cutting off a girl's clitoris and labia and sometimes sewing what remains together (except for space for menstrual blood to flow out) is intended as a way to prove the virginity of the girl or woman when taken in marriage, perhaps as one of many wives. This mutilation, of course, also assures that first penetration must tear through scar tissue, that intercourse can never be pleasurable, and that childbirth will be painful. Pulitzer Prize-winning author and feminist (or, her preference, "womanist") Alice Walker has galvanized public opinion against FMG through her writingand film collaboration with Pratibha Parmar on *Warrior Marks* (1993). When Walker was interviewed, she confronted her critics with this ringing statement: "Torture is not culture!" repudiating the right to do this to little girls in the name of religion and culture.

Supportive, Protective, Egalitarian Men

In one version of Atalanta's myth, hunters who think they are rescuing her kill the mother bear. In another version (preferred by readers who feel a connection with bears and Atalanta), the hunters come upon Atalanta when she is alone in the bear's cave and take her back to their camp. In both versions, Atalanta is, for a time, raised by men, from whom she learns language and proficiency with bow and arrows and spear. She no doubt gets approval and encouragement from these men, taking to everything they teach. Atalanta would have felt special, cared for, and supported during this phase of her life, as do girls in the mold of Artemis who have fathers who are delighted with their spunk and abilities.

It is easy to think of Atalanta as a high-spirited, confident girl who, small as she is, stands toe to toe with these hunters, insisting on what she thinks is true and protesting when something is not fair. Men like these take pride in such daughters. They are "Daddy's best buddy" or "Daddy's little girl." This kind of relationship often comes to an end as puberty approaches and it's time to establish physical and emotional distance from the budding woman the daughter is becoming. This transition may go smoothly or may be tempestuous and fraught with emotional outbursts. A best-buddy phase with a father who is admired and a good role model supports give-and-take, encourages assertiveness, and recognizes developing skills. These young women tend to become like their fathers or father figures in certain ways that give them a sense of pride, because their fathers are proud of them.

In *The Hunger Games* (Collins, 2008), Katniss Everdeen is sixteen when the trilogy begins. The happiest time in the week for her is when she goes with her father into the woods, lakes, and meadows outside the District-12 fence, beyond which citizens are forbidden to go. There, he teaches her to hunt with a bow and arrow, to bring down food for the family, and to hunt game to trade. Katniss has both instinct and skill; her arrows fly where she sends them. After her father's death, Katniss becomes the sole provider for her mother and sister. Her mother withdraws into her grief and stops functioning, and it is up to Katniss to look after the family.

Both Atalanta and Katniss excel as hunters, taught by their fathers or father figures to be competent and survive on their own. Katniss clearly identifies with her father and takes over as provider and protector as much as she can at his death. Her mother is clearly not a role model. In fact, both Atalanta's and Katniss' mothers are ineffectual. And, although Atalanta's father rejects her and orders her exposed on a mountaintop to die, in psychological terms, both are "fathers' daughters." They are women who are decisive, can act swiftly, choose targets or goals of their own, and have the focus and skill to hit what they aim for. Their worlds are outside the household that is the realm of "mothers' daughters."

In the United States toward the end of the 1960s and 1970s, consciousness-raising groups became the foundation of the Women's Movement. Here, women learned about sexism and inequality. They became determined that this had to change, and they encouraged each other to make a difference. Women shared information, wrote, marched, testified, had demonstrations, and entered formerly all-male enclaves and professions. *Ms.* magazine began publication. Couples worked to create egalitarian relationships and families. As a result, girls with Artemis qualities circa 1970 and after were likely to have parental approval to be active and confident. Spirited three-year-old girls with minds of their own could express what they wanted and felt, and still bask in the approval of their fathers and mothers. No more Little Miss Muffetts sitting on tuffets eating her curds and whey. Now, far from being frightened away by the spider, these emanicipated girls could be free to investigate and explore all the critters and creatures in the outdoors with interest. Indeed, little *Ms.* Muffett was "free to be you and me," and sang the songs to prove it!

Send Word, Bear Mother

Helen Stoltzfus, author of and principal performer in the award-winning documentary film *Send Word, Bear Mother* (*www.theoi.com*), based her work on her own true story, a saga that began with her illness and infertility. She had seen many specialists without success over many years. With symptoms of fatigue and infertility, and no satisfactory explanations for either, Helen joined a support group for people with life-threatening and chronic illnesses. In an exercise in which she was supposed to tap into inner sources of healing and imagination, a skeptical Helen unexpectedly began having a series of profound encounters with a mother grizzly bear spirit who appeared to her in dreams and came to her unbidden in fantasy. She experienced these as powerful visitations from the spirit world. They empowered her to try one more specialist in her effort to get pregnant.

This doctor diagnosed Helen as having endometriosis—a condition in which cells that are part of the lining of the uterus that are normally shed during menstruation can grow anywhere in the peritoneum (the space that holds all our internal organs below the diaphragm)—and recommended surgery. Helen had the surgery, but there seemed to be no satisfactory explanation for her condition. So she began to search for possible causes. She learned that environmental toxins, dioxins in particular, had been linked to endometriosis. Meanwhile, the mother grizzly bear visitations continued. This prodded her to learn all she could about bears, including that bears are threatened by the same toxins as humans.

The bear-mother spirit persisted relentlessly in Helen's psyche, calling her to go to Alaska where the bears live. As soon after her surgery as she could, she heeded the call and went to Denali National Park by herself. She did not feel well. The effects of chronic fatigue and the operation had sapped her energy, and travel took even more out of her.

She went, like sick people going to Lourdes, with the hope of being healed. Immediately upon entering the park, a mother grizzly with two cubs walked across the road in front of the tour bus. (In Denali, tourists are driven on buses through the park, while bears roam freely.) This was like a powerful waking dream to Helen. The real and the symbolic came together. While Helen may have appeared to be just another tourist, for her this was truly a pilgrimage.

No logical or practical decision brought Helen to Alaska, but rather a persistent and compelling message to come. The mother-bear symbol showed up over and over—not just in dreams and thoughts, but also in outer experiences. Helen encountered bear images in various art forms and in references in conversations. Suddenly, the idea or symbol of bear seemed to be everywhere. The urge or compelling desire to see real bears in their natural setting grew and set her on course for Denali. Only after going to Alaska did she come to understand the connection between what toxins had done to her body and the similar dangers they held for bears—as well as the larger implication of the danger to the wilderness and to Mother Nature herself.

The spirit of the bear gave an urgency to Helen's desire to do something with her new knowledge. She found her means of expression in her work. She wrote and staged a one-woman performance piece that became the basis for the film *Send Word, Bear Mother,* in which she played the principal role. Through this film and in the work that came from her inner/outer journey, Helen became an activist with a personal mission to foster an awareness of the connection between toxins, infertility, and the danger of the disappearing wilderness. And what's more, she became pregnant one month after she came back from Denali. Nine months later, her daughter, Lydia, was born.

"Send Word, Bear Mother" was Helen's personal healing chant, one that she adapted from a Sioux chant.

Send word, bear mother
Send word, bear mother
I'm having a hard time
Send word, bear mother

Send word, bear mother
I'm having a bad time.

Helen's encounters with the mother-bear spirit had a she-who-must-be-obeyed energy about them that persisted until she heeded the message, went to Alaska, and saw real bear mothers. The bear had a grip on her imagination. The chant was a plea for help to the bear-mother spirit—for healing.

Christine is another woman who had a profound encounter with mother bear, who came to her in a dream. In this dream, her arm was held in the jaws of a powerful mother bear who would not let go. She could neither shake the bear off nor get help from men in the dream. Then she came to a large, familiar statue of a mother bear with two cubs that she had often seen at the University of California Medical Center. In her dream, when she placed her hands on the statue, the bear finally let go of her arm.

As we talked about her dream, Christine intuitively connected her recent obsession about having a baby with the mother bear. She kept noticing pregnant women and women with babies; intrusive thoughts about becoming pregnant herself came into her mind and were followed by anxiety. She wanted and feared this. She had her course set on becoming a psychologist. She had only a year left to finish the academic preparation, after which she wanted to begin a practice. Now the idea of having a baby intruded and she felt that, if she gave in to it, it would mean sacrificing her career. When we explored what putting her hands on the statue of the mother bear could mean, she had a strong sense that, by doing so, she was making a promise. With the promise made, the bear could let her go.

After this discussion with me, Christine went home and told her husband about the dream and its meaning to her. In their talk, they decided that, once she finished her last year of school, their goal would be for her to become pregnant. They would share childcare responsibilities and support each other's work. With Christine's husband backing up her promise to mother bear, her intrusive, obsessive thoughts went away. The mother bear let go the grip she had on Christine's psyche once she felt an inner certainty that she would honor the mother bear in herself.

Bears and Women

"Undressing the Bear" is a chapter in Terry Tempest Williams' *An Unspoken Hunger: Stories from the Field* (1995). In it, Williams tells bear stories, relates dreams of bears, and shares anecdotes that point to a connection between women and bears. She writes:

> *We are creatures of paradox, women and bears, two animals that are enormously unpredictable, hence our mystery. Perhaps the fear of bears and the fear of women lies*

in our refusal to be tamed, the impulses we arouse and the forces we represent.

Among the stories in this particular chapter, there is a description of a bear dream from a bookseller friend of Terry's who tells of sharing it with a male customer:

"I dreamt I was in Yellowstone. A grizzly, upright, was walking toward me. Frightened at first, I began to pull away, when suddenly a mantle of calm came over me. I walked toward the bear and we embraced." The man across the counter listened, and then said matter-of-factly, "Get over it."

Terry mused: "Why? Why should we give up the dream of embracing the bear? For me, it has everything to do with undressing, exposing, and embracing the Feminine." She explains:

I see the Feminine defined as a reconnection to the Self, a commitment to the wildness within—our instincts, our capacity to create and destroy; our hunger for connection as well as sovereignty, interdependence and independence, at once. We are taught not to trust our own experience.

It is interesting that the ferocious protective power of the bear is an attribute of Artemis and not of the Greek mother goddesses, who were powerless to protect themselves or their children from male predators and abusive partners. In fact, in Greek mythology and in the history of the Western civilization that owes so much to the Greeks, women have neither been empowered nor equal to men, however Olympian their social status. Gaia, the personification of earth who birthed all life on the planet, is abused by her husband,

Uranus, after he grows increasingly resentful of her fertility. When he prevents anything further from being born, she is in great pain, until her son, Cronos, emasculates his father and consigns him to the deepest and darkest part of the underworld, replacing him as the chief god. Rhea, the mother of the Olympians, stands by helplessly as her husband, Cronos, fearing that he will have a son who will do to him what he did to his own father, swallows her first five children as soon as they are born. Finally, in her sixth pregnancy, Rhea wraps a stone in swaddling clothes and tricks him into believing he has swallowed Zeus, who grows to manhood and, with allies, overthrows his father. Demeter, the mother of Persephone, can not prevent her daughter's abduction and rape.

Good human mothers mirror their children, respond to their happy or sad emotions, and realize that their children's feelings matter. They see their individuality, their strengths, and their sensitivities. Between a healthy mother and child, there is a reciprocity and response that fosters the growth of emotional intelligence.

This is not what mother bears do. Girls in the mold of Atalanta are often very independent, but not very good at intimacy with friends or partners. The forging of emotional bonds becomes challenging to them and to those who love them. Intimacy grows through mirroring, reciprocity, empathy, compassion, and thoughtfulness. Atalanta the adult may be a woman who did not learn how to look after the feelings of others and who may not know her own emotional needs or feelings. She can not learn this from bear mother/Mother Nature or the Artemis archetype. This she can only learn from other human beings.

Chapter Three

ATALANTA AND MELEAGER

In marked contrast to the rejection and rage of Arcadia's king at Atalanta's birth, Meleager's birth is greeted with jubilation and celebration by all. In fact, Meleager's first accomplishment is to be born a boy. But the expectations placed upon Meleager from the moment of his birth also have consequences. As a first-born son with good lineage, position, and wealth, he enters a world of privilege and is expected to carry on the family tradition.

Assumptions about who a newborn will grow up to be are made by parents, extended family, religions, social classes, and cultures. These assumptions can be changed or challenged if there is social mobility, universal education, and democracy in the historical time and place in which the child is born. Most people in the world today do not have the opportunity to make their own choices based on their innate predispositions or talents, or for love of what they do, or love for a particular person. And while this is especially true for daughters raised in places and families where patriarchal and fundamentalist religious attitudes limit them, it also has an effect on sons that often is not appreciated. Boys may be greatly valued over daughters, they may be more likely to be educated and have more social freedom, yet they too must conform to societal norms. Physical punishment or shame enforces acceptable behavior in boys as well as girls.

Psychological Abandonment

Atalanta is physically abandoned and expected to die. The harsh reality is that many unwanted girls face a similar fate today. However, boys are often not free to grow up to be the men they want to be either, especially if they are princes—metaphorically or actually. Meleager, like Prince Charles and now Prince William of England, is expected to take on the role to which he is born, as are many of the sons of political or business leaders today. If that role isn't a good psychological fit, it can result in an emotionally abandoned child whose own dreams do not matter in the psyche of the man. This may also be true for the sons of immigrants who enjoy great opportunities and so must fulfill high expectations. And it may be true for the son whose purpose is to be the successful athlete that his father aspired to be. When sons who are drawn to create art, play music, or make things with their hands are born into families where intellectual and financial achievement is what matters, they often find themselves abandoning interests dear to them in order to be accepted and valued.

I developed the concept of the "abandoned child" when I wrote *Ring of Power* (1992). This inner child is an archetype when a son or daughter is expected to be an extension of a parent's needs, ambitions, or unfulfilled life. It arises when a child is not seen as an individual who comes into the world to live a unique life of his or her own. It is illustrated by the story of a three-generation dysfunctional family in Richard Wagner's *Ring Cycle,* the four operas that comprise *Der Ring des Nibelungen: Das Rheingold, Die Walküre, Siegfried,* and *Gotterdammerung,* and it appears in the lives of people who have similar family dynamics. In this powerful archetypal story set to magnificent music, Wotan is the counterpart of Zeus. He makes decisions about his children, prescribes their roles, and values them as tools through which they may acquire the ring of power after which he lusts.

In today's world, the ring of power can symbolize money, fame, political power, prestige, defeating a rival or triumphing over an enemy, or furthering an ambition for power and acceptance beyond wealth. This was the case for Joseph Kennedy, founding father of a family that was seen, for a time, as the equivalent of an American royal family.

Kennedy's sons were groomed to become presidents of the United States. By doing so, they would acquire power and respectability beyond that enjoyed by those who looked down upon their father's own immigrant, Irish Catholic beginnings. Eldest son Joe was the one expected to bring this prize to his father, but he was shot down in the Second World War. Then it was up to the next son, John F. Kennedy, whose natural bent was not in this direction, to take up this quest. When John was elected and then assassinated, it fell to his younger brother, Robert, to deliver the prize. In his bid to gain the presidential nomination, he, too, was assassinated.

In families ruled over by an ambitious parent, children learn that approval is conditional; it depends on conforming to expectations. This can be due to pressure from either a father or a mother. Success matters, whether demonstrated through friends, schools, sports, or grades. The impression the child makes must reflect well on the parent and further his or her ambitions. Getting into the right schools and clubs or marrying well are expectations. When children's psyches become focused on getting approval or fulfilling their parents' ambitions, they lose what might otherwise have mattered to them personally. What might otherwise have been a source of joy and satisfaction to them is forgotten or left undeveloped.

Something similar happens to children who learn not to grieve people or pets that disappear from their lives. It could have been a housekeeper or some other employee, who spent more love and time with the child than anyone else, or the child next door who moves away, or someone special who is now estranged from the parent and doesn't visit anymore. This was someone who did matter, that the youngster is not supposed to miss or mention. Later, as adolescents, they may be driven to give up a socially inappropriate friend and, by doing so, betray their own capacity for friendship as well as the other person. When signs of growing personhood are suppressed from fear of losing approval or being humiliated, children lose touch with their own ideas, interests, and preferences, and learn to silence voices to the contrary in themselves. As a result, an "abandoned child" may reside in the adults they become.

Meleager As a Greek Hero

As a boy and a young man, Meleager is well-suited to his position, his culture, and his time. He is a physically active boy whose all-consuming interest lies in hunting.

His proud father has miniature bow and arrows and spear made for him with which he practices hour after hour, honing his skills. As a prince, he joins his father's men on hunts and, at an early age, becomes an expert hunter. This obsessive fascination with mastery seems to arise in some boys who have an innate aptitude for a sport (or today, it could be a videogame) and an ability not to be distracted. Some sports—golf, tennis, skiing, surfing, mountain biking, high diving—require both intensity on the part of the boy and access to facilities. Some sports entail risking physical harm with each increment in difficulty or complexity—skateboarding stunts, for instance. Taking risks requires courage (or foolhardiness), something young men who identify with the hero and who have no sense of their own mortality have in abundance. Boys and young men who have been singled out as special may be further motivated by their fathers' or father figures' approval.

In ancient Greece—as in some parts of the non-industrial, patriarchal developing world, and in competitive sports—approval and fame came from physical achievement. By the time he is a young man, Meleager is known as the best hunter in ancient Greece. His trophies are the pelts of animals, enough to cover the floors of the huge castle. His natural abilities, his bravery, and his skill as a hunter are admired. He answers Jason's invitation to sail as an Argonaut on the quest for the Golden Fleece, a quest that attracted the heroes, demigods, and nobles of all Greece. The lure was glory and adventure. The Argo was the largest and most elaborate ship that had yet been designed. The goddess Athena fitted a beam into the prow made from the speaking oaks of the grove at Dodona where Zeus had his oracle. Though the lists differ as to who the fifty heroes were who went on this mythological expedition, which took place a generation before the Trojan War, some of the names included are familiar as the fathers of the heroes in the *Iliad*.

Meleager and His Mother

When Atropos tied the fate of Meleager to the smoldering end of a burning log, she gave the queen the power to control her son's destiny. The biology and psychology of infancy similarly gives to a mere mortal woman—often a young one—the power of life or death over her child. In the beginning of a newborn's life, its survival depends upon basic maternal care. In the early weeks and months of life, survival can depend upon loving maternal contact. In medical school, I learned that babies separated from their mothers to protect them from the London Blitzkrieg suffered from anaclitic depression and died, even though they got good basic physical care. They were kept warm and fed, and had their diapers changed, but many didn't survive. It seems that infants who are not held and cherished, who do not hear their mother's voice or feel her body or her breath may die for lack of maternal loving care. One could perhaps say that they die of a broken heart.

Failure to thrive is a common diagnosis for older babies and toddlers who are underweight or listless. Many of these children have been neglected by their birth mothers, who are often practically children themselves, or who are suffering from extended post-partum depression, or who have had too many children to look after another. Likewise, there are children (most often girls) who are not vaccinated against common diseases or brought to a doctor when they are sick. Many of these die of readily treated illnesses or suffer from malnutrition, especially in instances where poverty and patriarchy decide who in the family gets the food.

Whatever the circumstances, to a baby, the mother *is* the environment. Mother either provides or does not. Her size relative to the baby is enormous. She is all-powerful, all-providing, or all-withholding. She is the embodiment of the Great Mother in a pre-verbal world—an archetype in the unconscious of men that helps explain the efforts that men make to control women and their irrational fear of them. Thus, the power over Meleager's life that Atropos gives to his mother has a reality in human infancy and early childhood.

However, as boys grow up, their mothers' life-or-death power becomes metaphoric rather than real, relating primarily to the development of their emotional lives. Alice Miller, in her book *The Drama of the Gifted Child* (Basic Books, 1981), describes how boys can learn to pay attention to their mothers' emotional needs and to respond in ways that will soothe them, at the expense of their own feelings. They learn to attend to their mothers' moods and needs. A narcissistically wounded mother wants her little man to be her mirror, not to express his own feelings or challenge her. The emotionally absent or distant father who is not available to either his wife or his son may be complicit in fostering an emotionally incestuous relationship that takes on the metaphoric configuration of Great Mother/Son Lover, which was a phase in pre-patriarchal religions and is an archetypal relationship.

It is important that some mothers and some sons recognize this pattern in order to change it. This may not have been necessary for Meleager, who, from the beginning, "hung out" among men and emulated them. Boys like him are outer-oriented, interested in things rather than people, and competitive. If physically coordinated and athletic, they compete in sports. The Apollo archetype fits Meleager—God of the Sun who is the favorite son of Zeus and twin to Artemis; the embodiment of a masculine attitude that observes, favors thinking over feeling, competes with his intelligence, and strives for excellence; a person with an innate discipline to practice at whatever he needs to master to reach a goal or win. While Meleager will not be a "mother's son"—overly close to her and sensitive to her feelings more than his own—he may become an extension of her social ambitions through the plans she makes for him.

By the time Meleager reaches manhood, he has easily met the expectations of his father. But his mother has expectations and needs for him to fulfill as well. He must marry someone appropriate in her eyes, and she expects him to make a choice from among the young women she selects. In a patriarchy, women live through their relationships with men. They have status by virtue of being someone's daughter, until they become wives and then the mothers of sons. When they are widowed, they are immediately diminished in importance, although, at least in ancient Greece, they were not expected to join their dead husbands on the funeral pyre. In a system like this, it is the relationship of a mother to her son that matters. And to this end, it is important that the son's wife be respectful, if not indebted, to her mother-in-law.

Ambition takes many forms. Where women cannot themselves aspire to power or prestige, they live their ambitions out through their sons or husbands. Sons may be molded to become the men their mothers wanted to be.

Since the Women's Movement, it is possible for women to succeed in almost any field or profession. This reality recalls Gloria Steinem's famous comment: "We are becoming the men we were supposed to marry."

That mothers live through their sons is, however, still true. While this happens across the social spectrum, it is often more pronounced in immigrant families and among those at the top of the social ladder. Social class and inherited wealth make it likely that a married woman will be a full-time wife and mother, even if she is brighter and more able than her husband. Such women can be frustrated by thwarted ambitions of their own, especially if their husbands turn out to be failures in contrast to their wives' more successful fathers. Now that women are able to rise to the top of corporations, professions, elected offices, and even the armed services, this is changing. Women no longer have to live through the accomplishments of others. A woman no longer has to be "the woman behind the throne" if she has what it takes herself.

Atalanta and Meleager—Twinning Couple

Of all the versions of the story of Atalanta, I find Bernard Evslin's narrative (*Heroes, Gods, and Monsters*, 1968) about how Meleager and Atalanta met not only the most vivid, but also the most psychologically true explanation of their attraction. In my own telling, I borrow the situation that brought them together from him and then interpret the story so that it makes internal psychological sense. In classical Greek and Roman versions, the circumstances given differ greatly; but in all of them, Meleager falls in love with

Atalanta at first sight. She evokes an image, a yearning for a feminine counterpart—his dream girl or *anima* figure, in Jung's psychological model. When men talk about attractive women, their first comment usually focuses on their appearance or on particular physical attributes.

Atalanta and Meleager are a standout matched set—a striking couple, both archers and hunters at home in the wilderness. Atalanta evokes Artemis, twin sister to Apollo. She has her silver bow, he his golden one. This twinning is a characteristic of many young relationships that become marriages. In high school, the football captain and the head cheerleader or prom queen are the classic couple. In colleges where "the Greeks" dominate social life, sorority sisters find their match in fraternity brothers—and back in the days before couples lived together, this often led to marriage after graduation.

Even now, when couples marry late, after both have put career or higher education before marriage, "twinning" can be seen in the look-alike couples in the engagement photographs in the Sunday *New York Times*. These couples are brought together by shared interests and values, and by friends they have in common. They meet at conferences or other venues that provide opportunities for people in the same fields to foster relationships based on friendships and comraderie built during those early career years following college. Online dating websites encourage people who have affinities to meet; social networking gives information on background, education, and friends held in common, although living in many other locations. Men and women increasingly form couples in which each describes the other as "best friend." They share passions and can be competitive—in sports, or as cooks and foodies. They may take on a shared spiritual practice or work out together. They may be entrepreneurs. In other words—especially if they are successful at what they do—they may become a Meleager/Atalanta couple, an Artemis/Apollo couple. As such, they take on the next phase of adulthood together, often along with others in their age cohort. Romance and mystery are often missing when each seems so familiar to the other—like a brother or sister with whom one has sex and children.

Romance—falling head over heels in love—is a phase of attraction in which there is a magnetic pull to a stranger who embodies an unconscious dream of merger, completeness, or wholeness with a goddess. When a man like Meleager sees his dream girl, beauty is in the eye and heart of the beholder. His initial response is echoed in the words to "Some Enchanted Evening"—something about "seeing a stranger across a crowded room" and somehow knowing to "never let her go." The woman who is the recipient of this infatuation, especially if she is an Atalanta, is not initially impressed and may be annoyed, thinking: "He doesn't know me; how can he say he loves me!" However, if a relationship grows past this initial impression, the two may marvel at how each is a reverse-gender version of the other. Often it is the male who cares more.

In the long-running television series *Bones*, the protagonist, Dr. Temperance Brennan, is a brilliant forensic anthropologist. With her knowledge of and fascination for bones and the information she can glean from them, she helps solve how people died and hunts for their murderers with her partner, Seeley Booth, an FBI agent with a strong sense of people. Physically, Booth is a Meleager to Brennan's Atalanta. Brennan is often unaware of the feelings of those around her and inept at appropriate emotional responses. She is fearless and excels in self-defense. She was abandoned when her parents disappeared and she entered the system as a foster child. Making her way in that wilderness, she learned not to trust what could not be verified scientifically.

Booth and Brennan are partners on the hunt. Each is best at what they do. Like Atalanta and Meleager, they are a remarkable pair. Like them, they are a couple that mutually admires what each excels at and can do. For men and women who relate as colleagues—as competitors and equals in the workplace, in universities, in explorations and challenges—these relationships are based on personal affinities. Family ties, ethnicity, and social class often cease to be important to them. Parental expectations go by the wayside. They are not doing what they were expected to do. Meleager's mother was especially vexed by this, and parents with high expectations of couples who form similar relationships may be as well.

Chapter Four

THE HUNT FOR THE CALYDON BOAR

It is a common theme in Greek mythology that to offend a god or goddess has very serious consequences. In the myth of Atalanta, the offense was to Artemis, who is outraged when Meleager's father gives thanks and offers sacrifices to myriad gods and goddesses, including the country gods and all the gods of the Heavens, and leaves her out. Much of Calydon was a forested wilderness rich with wildlife—Artemis' favorite terrain. So, in retribution, she creates the huge boar of the myth and unleashes it to ravage the countryside.

When people believed that the world was inhabited by divinities, events beyond their control or understanding were seen as punishment brought on by some offense, usually to a male god. Zeus brought storms and lightning down on people; Poseidon unleashed earthquakes and huge waves as an expression of his anger. Hera usually directed her jealousy toward a particular woman, but once unleashed her destructive wrath on the whole island of Aegina. Attributing disasters to offended gods and goddesses was a means of making sense of otherwise irrational events. History and religion are full of examples in which sacrifices were made to appease an angry god, or punishment was meted out for bringing on drought, crop failure, economic recession, or plague.

Destructive Rage in Families

Living with a Calydon boar remains vividly real in dysfunctional families in which a powerful adult can go out of control—a parent who erupts into rage or behaves as if possessed, becoming a different person when under the influence of an intoxicant, or in fear or anger. Male rage that results in domestic violence against wives and children is common and frightening. CDC statistics show that one out of four women experience domestic violence in their lifetimes. Nearly three out of four Americans (74 percent) know someone personally who is or has been a victim of domestic violence.

Imagine (or remember) being small and dependent, at the mercy of a parent who towers over you—a giant figure who, on becoming disturbed by something, suddenly becomes enraged. A young child who lives in a dysfunctional family with a bipolar, borderline, post-traumatic-stress-syndrome or rageaholic parent lives in an emotional landscape that resembles this mythical world in which mortals live their lives in relationship to powerful Olympians. In families like these, a little girl can be punished for not doing something beyond her abilities. In one household, a father demanded that his daughter make him a cup of coffee; when she couldn't and tried to say so, she was backhanded and told that she was no good. In another, a boy was whipped for crying and told he would now have something to cry about!

In the story of the Calydon boar, it is a goddess whose rage is devastating, just as a furious mother's outbursts can be to a small child. Women are responsible for 15 percent of domestic violence reports in the United States.

The mythical and patriarchal world of classical Greece was violent from the beginning. It was driven by a cosmology where fathers and grown sons fought for power, and in which rape and incest were common. Once Zeus became chief god, he ruled from Olympus through fear with his thunderbolts. Likewise, fear of judgment and punishment from above is a source of fear or dread in many adults. If they surpass a parent, differ in values, or challenge a fundamental religious belief, they live in a state of "waiting for lightning to strike." This is an archetypal pattern when it is lived out in a home or country headed by a punitive and unpredictable despot whose word is law.

The Calydon Boar As Inner Symbol

The enormous boar that an outraged Artemis sent to devastate the Calydon countryside, when the king honored other divinities, but not her, was vividly described in Bulfinch's Mythology: "Its eyes shone with blood and fire, its bristles stood like threatening spears, its tusks were like those of Indian elephants. The growing corn was trampled, the vines and olive trees laid waste, the flocks and herds were driven in wild confusion. People fled behind walls, the only hope of safety."

This ravening beast is a powerful negative symbol of Artemis. Other symbols of her, like the stag or quail, have a "now you see them, now you don't" elusiveness about them. The bear can be ferocious, but this is an aspect of a protective mother that comes out when her young are threatened. The Calydon boar, however, has no redeeming qualities. It is deliberately created by Artemis to cause damage in her rage at being snubbed or unacknowledged. Once it comes to life and begins ravaging the countryside, it is out of control.

When a woman with a cause becomes so outraged that she is out of control and can't see that this is damaging both her cause and herself (as well as innocent others), she has been taken over by her Calydon boar. She doesn't care who or what her words or actions hurt. Hers is an outrage that begins with a sense of entitlement—she is somebody of significance and value who has been dismissed as inconsequential. How dare they! Or she acts as an avenger of injustice who brings retribution. She, someone she loves, or something she values has been treated with disrespect or abused. She will get even! Her Calydon boar anger grows out of all proportion.

Justification and righteousness are like the impervious pelt of the boar, the thick skin of defensive armor that protects against barbs of criticism. An outraged woman does not recognize the person she has become or realize that the centered, fair-witness part of herself has been trampled underfoot and is a casualty of her own righteous anger. This dynamic obviously applies to men as well, who usually (because of patriarchy) have a greater sense of entitlement and are therefore more susceptible to feeling humiliated.

The Calydon boar may take over a woman's inner life when she suppresses a seething rage, thus destroying her own inner landscape. There is no peace inside her; she no longer sees the beauty of nature around her; she is annoyed by her beloved animals; she puts a wall up between herself and others and wants to be left alone. It could be that her anger, compounded by her strength of will, prevents her from feeling grief and disappointment, which keeps tears from welling up. She fears looking weak or emotional. Hidden under her anger, provoked by whatever set it off, she may be harboring a reservoir of anger and grief, a yearning to be valued and loved. If Artemis hadn't been slighted, and instead had been honored and valued or even loved, she would not have unleashed the boar on Calydon.

To be full of rage, to harbor hostile thoughts toward others, to be obsessed by slights, is harmful to the psyche of the person who has these feelings. A dream helped one woman begin to understand this. She told me that work was not going well. She had begun at a new position for which she was well qualified; she could handle what she was hired to do with relative ease. The problem was with co-workers. She had gotten off on a wrong note, somehow. She felt that they talked behind her back and were resentful when she made suggestions. Her academic credentials were superior to theirs, and she had more experience. She found herself belittling them in her mind and was preoccupied by imaginary conversations in which "she showed them!"

In this woman's dream, she was in a familiar country church. She stepped outside to find two large dogs who snarled and attacked her, going for her throat. At first, she equated the dogs with her co-workers. But in talking about the slights, she realized that it would be a gross exaggeration to say that this is how they were intended. Moreover, the attack stood in contrast to the peaceful feelings she had in the church. It was when she left this symbol of the Self—or spiritual center—that the dogs attacked. She was open to the possibility that the dogs could represent both an exaggerated perception of her co-workers and something in herself that could get paranoid and was destructive to her. If they were "her" dogs, then they endangered her. She found that this insight gave her the choice of taking deep breaths and centering, or getting all worked up by her own thoughts. Once she changed her inner world, the atmosphere in her outer world at work gradually changed as well, as did her dreams.

If this woman had gone to work day after day thinking the worst of the others in her office, belittling them because she felt that she deserved the respect of her position and education, the office staff would naturally have spent as little time around her as possible and not included her in the informal camaraderie of people who work together. Worse still, if she continued to live with mental attack dogs as inner company—if she nursed slights and hostile thoughts—she risked becoming a bitter woman.

When you feed the attack dogs in your mind, you make them more powerful and destructive to your soul and relationships. The off-centeredness that goes with this affects your judgment about the situation, about others, and about yourself.

No one is ever her usual or best self when an "attack dog" complex takes over and is consequently obsessed by envy, or dwells upon slights, or harbors hostile or paranoid feelings about the thoughts or motives of others. An "attack dog" is a powerful metaphor that has the same meaning as the Calydon boar. It's that part in the psyche that reacts with defensive hostility, when it attacks others in anger. It has to be faced and disempowered by the woman in which it lives. It can be transformed through developing discernment and restraint in the present plus insight and compassion into its origins in the past. What remains are the protective qualities of Artemis, which is like a companion dog that has good instincts to sniff out real danger, is a protector of boundaries, guardian of the one-in-herself virgin goddess archetype in a woman's psyche, and defender of vulnerable others: a good dog!

The Calling of the Hunt

Calydon's king calls upon the heroes and would-be heroes of Greece to come on a great hunt to kill the boar. These are by nature aggressive men used to taking what they can by force. As they assemble, the king begins to feel uneasy about going on the hunt and leaving his castle unguarded. Yet he fears that, if he doesn't go on the hunt, Meleager may be at risk. The loss of his heir would endanger the kingdom. When he voices this quandary to the queen, she assures him that he can stay in the castle and doesn't have to worry about Meleager. She shows him the hidden chest that contains the partially burned log and tells him the story of Atropos' visit.

To volunteer to join the boar hunt is a call to adventure, a chance for fame, and a test of physical courage. Like Jason's quest for the Fleece or, a generation later, Agamemnon's expedition to Troy, it is a challenge for men only. Atalanta is the exception. Now, women can be astronauts, or soldiers and officers in armed conflicts. They can form expeditions to climb mountains—those who do are likely to have Artemis as a major archetype and be similar to Atalanta. But even today, these women run into resentment and the risk of rape from some men who think they do not belong with them. Women who think that they are accepted as "one of the boys"—as equals to men—often find out that this is not the case.

The story of the hunt is told in great detail by all the classical writers. They all give the names of the men in a long roll call, including mention of the sons they will later father, as for Peleus, the father of Achilles. They give a blow-by-blow narrative of what they do—to no avail. Some are gored, trampled, or slashed by the boar's tusks. Their weapons, deflected off the thick hide of the boar, sometimes wound others. The wiley boar stays hidden at first, and then explosively charges out from behind a grove of willows as the hunters pass close by his hiding place. The boar chooses a strategic location. The hunters can neither surround it nor mass an attack; they have to attack singly or in pairs.

Atalanta holds her ground as the boar charges toward her. She has to stop the boar or it will destroy her. It takes courage to hold steady and aim true, and to fire the arrow that enters the boar's eye and penetrates its brain. The boar staggers, and Meleager delivers the death blow with his sword.

Atalanta's Confrontation with the Boar

By facing the boar, Atalanta faces the destructive aspect of Artemis. For women who are archetypally similar, this is a confrontation with the shadow in themselves. A woman who feels righteous anger at indifference toward what is sacred to her is susceptible to being taken over by outrage and losing all sense of proportion or compassion. She becomes possessed by the boar when she acts like one herself and makes anyone who tries to reason with her an enemy. What begins in her as compassionate action to save girls and women—or as deep ecological concern for deforestation and pollution of the environment, or her heartfelt response to witnessing cruelty to animals—becomes blind rage that consumes her and threatens the very humanity that is the source of her concern for vulnerable others.

It takes courage to confront the inner boar, for doing so means that a woman must confront her own destructiveness directly. To do so, she has to see—better yet, feel—how much damage she has done to herself and others by trampling on their feelings, or on what they have been tending that she did not value. She needs to feel remorse for the contempt and judgment she unleashed on others in the past, and realize that only she can stop it. With this intention and determination, she can rein in those feelings. Whether in a family matter or a global one, to become an avenging goddess is a bad thing for a woman and for those around her—who are, after all, not all bad, as she tends to feel once she gets worked up. Insight into this behavior often uncovers an underlying attitude of superiority and arrogance, which are the very qualities she finds intolerable in others. Confronting the inner boar can become a lesson in humility.

There is a line in T. S. Eliot's *Four Quartets* that an arrogant woman or an alpha male would do well to understand:

the only wisdom we can hope to acquire
is the wisdom of humility

The Boar As a Destructive Force of Nature

In failing to honor and sacrifice to the sacred feminine represented by Artemis, the king brings destruction down on his kingdom. The people and the land suffer from an indiscriminate force of nature, symbolized by the boar, that destroys everything in its path. This same patriarchal mindset—which fails to honor the sacred feminine, fails to protect the planet and all life on it, and to make sacrifices to sustain what we have—is resulting now in the indiscriminate consequences of climate and weather change.

Tornados in the Midwest have been tearing up everything in their paths, wreaking havoc and returning to do more of the same, leaving behind devastation that resembles that done by the boar. Likewise floods, hurricanes, drought, forest fires, and rising seas are indicators of climate change that is happening because we cease to honor our relationship to a living planet. Gaia, Mother Nature, Mother Earth, are aspects of the sacred feminine or Great Goddess, who provides us with air, water, food, and beauty, out of which all things are born and into which they return. Like Artemis, Mother Nature reacts with destruction when there is no appreciation, no care-taking, no valuing or sacrifices made on her behalf.

Not enough trees, too many people is a simple equation that equals global warming and Calydon-boar effects. For Atalanta and Artemis, who are at home in forests—and for those of us who are "tree people"—trees are beautiful and have individual characteristics. Many live far longer than we ever will, and we recognize that trees and we ourselves are interdependent. Trees store carbon dioxide and transform it into nutrients and oxygen; they maintain the watershed by a root system that holds earth and water like a sponge that prevents floods, making more fertile earth as they compost their leaves. The arboreal and tropical rain forest—the lungs of the planet—are being clear-cut and are also catching fire. Behind this destruction is a shortsightedness and a desacralization of nature. Trees become so many board feet of lumber; forests are being replaced by cash crops like soybeans or palm oil.

I came to appreciate what trees do for us after losing an effort to save a beautiful Monterey pine in front of my house. In an area where morning fog is fairly common, pine needles distill the fog into drops of water to provide moisture to the plants and soil under the tree's canopy. Once this tree was cut down, I could see how it had been the center of a balanced ecological system. Besides teaching me about what trees do, the loss of this one tree led me to understand the difference between "tree people" and "not tree people." As a result of what I leaned, I wrote *Like a Tree: How Trees, Women, and Tree People Can Save the Planet* (2011).

For those who are not tree people, a tree is a thing, without intrinsic value. While the tree I tried to save was in front of my house, it was not on my property, but on "commons" held within a homeowners' association. Once a neighbor wanted it taken down, its fate depended on a vote and, in the rules and regulations of the association, preservation of scenic views had the highest priority. However it was a side view. The tree was there before any houses were and, for people who love trees, a tree can also provide a scenic view. Fear among association members was fanned by an urban legend that pine trees can explode in extreme heat, and this discussion was occurring in a wildland-urban interface area where fire hazards are taken seriously. Another argument was that, if the tree fell over or one of its branches fell and hurt someone, the association would be held liable. In the face of these concerns, the tree cutters prevailed.

In the time of classical mythology, most of Greece and Europe were covered with forests. Artemis' affinity for the woods did not require any effort to save them. But while this isn't part of her mythology, many women who share characteristics of Atalanta/Artemis are among those who save trees and forests. In India in the 1970s, the Chipko movement became the first successful movement in which women saved trees (*chipko* in Hindi means "tree huggers"). Twenty-seven women stopped deforestation by hugging the trees to prevent them from being cut down. An historical precedent occurred in 1730, when Amrita Devi and her three daughters were martyred rather than allow loggers to cut down a sacred *khejri* tree. Facing a charging boar and facing down angry loggers with bulldozers and axes takes courage. The spirit of Artemis was very much present in these activists.

THE DEATH OF MELEAGER

The arrow that Atalanta shot wounded but did not kill the boar. Because it is Meleager who deals the fatal blow, he is entitled to the pelt as a trophy. But instead of keeping it for himself, Meleager gives it to Atalanta, acknowledging that the two of them together had succeeded. The men, however, protest that this prize should not go to a woman. Meleager's two uncles demand that, if he wants to give the pelt away, it should go to them. One of them snatches at the pelt, but Meleager acts swiftly, swinging his sword and decapitating first one and then the other of his uncles. Their heads roll. There is no further protest, and everyone heads back to the castle for food and drink—except Atalanta and Meleager.

The hunting party tells the story of the hunt, and of how Atalanta's arrow drew first blood and Meleager killed the boar. Then they tell why and how Meleager killed his uncles. The queen is grief-stricken and furious, overcome by conflicting feelings. She grieves for her brothers and is appalled that Meleager killed them. She blames Atalanta. In her anger, she retrieves the partially burned log that Atropos showed her and orders the servants to build a pyre. In Ovid's *Metamorphoses,* the queen's despair and long soliloquy easily rival Hamlet's, showing the anguish she feels as mother and sister war within her. The sister wins. She throws the log into the fire, then drives a knife into her own heart, crying: "A death for a death, a crime for a crime, and trouble added and multiplied! So this cursed house shall go to ruin."

Meanwhile, Meleager and Atalanta linger in the familiarity of the wilderness, enjoying their love, their success, and their fame as a couple. Suddenly Meleager is overcome with a burning pain; he clutches his midsection and doubles over. And there, in the forest, he dies in Atalanta's arms.

Meleager and His Mother

Myth and life resemble one another when the power of life and death held by a man's mother is metaphoric and it is his emotional life over which she exercises control. Meleager's mother kills off the possibility that he can have a life with Atalanta. Many mothers do the same by manipulating their son's feelings, killing off a relationship by raising doubt, anxiety, responsibility, guilt, or shame.

Some readers may remember ending the love of their life or abandoning a soul mate after they were judged "unsuitable" or "inappropriate" or even "unnatural" by parents. The reasons for the opposition may have been differences in social class, religion, race, age, or gender-related. When pressure to adhere to family and cultural expectations is brought to bear on a son (and especially daughter), it is often the mother, who has been delegated by an assumption that is collectively held that it is her responsibility as a wife and mother to do this.

In real lives, a self-centered/narcissistic mother who believes that she knows best and knows more about her son's feelings than he does can raise him to be more aware of her feelings than his own. By the time he is a man, she can convince him that he should not trust himself to know who is the right mate for him. His tendency to acquiesce as an adult to what his mother says begins when he becomes the center of her emotional life beyond infancy and childhood. Maternal instinct bonds a mother to her baby and, for a time, a child's physical survival and growth depend upon being bonded to its mother. After a while, a normal tension develops between dependency and separation. From the time a child takes its first steps and learns to say "no," it is developing a separate sense of itself apart from its mother. This includes having its own feelings, which an emotionally needy or controlling mother may thwart.

In the absence of adult emotional and physical relationships, the mother of a boy may turn to him to meet her needs for closeness. As he grows older, she needs him to be her mirror to assure her that she is important and attractive. She may train him to be attuned to how she feels by praising him for his sensitivity and withholding affection, or by making him feel guilty for not paying attention to her when she wants it. He may learn to suppress his own feelings after being told time and time again that he should be ashamed for having them. A boy with a self-absorbed mother may find that he had better not cry when he is disappointed, or show anger toward her, or become excited about or express affection for others. When spontaneity, joy, anger, or grief can't be expressed in the presence of a powerful or needy parent, it goes elsewhere. Supressed grief may become sadness; anger may find an undeserving target; joy may be stifled.

A self-centered and psychologically needy mother makes everything about herself. A son's attributes and accomplishments seem to become hers—far beyond just "reflecting well on her." The difference between ordinary parental pride in a son or daughter and a psychologically unhealthy bond depends upon how much a parent is living through the child and whether the child is motivated primarily by pleasing the parent and avoiding the pain that comes with disapproval. A son with the intelligence to do so quickly learns what not to say. After a time, he learns not to pay attention to himself or to what he really feels or observes in others or about others. Emotional intelligence (EQ), like any other human ability, is favored or not by circumstance and is developed by encouragement and words that can communicate feelings and perception. Clear feeling, like clear thinking, does take practice.

Death and Dying in Myth and Dreams

In dreams as well as myths, people die. In our dreams, however, they are not characters from ancient myths; they are most likely people we know in our own lives, mixed with celebrities that are symbolic characters. It's not surprising, then, that dreams in which someone dies or is dead are often alarming, because our first inclination is to take the dreams literally. On awakening, the dreamer tries to check out the accuracy of the dream. Usually, it is not true; on rare occasions, however, it may be a telepathic or precognitive dream, which often has a different quality from normal dreams. Usually, the dream signals a symbolic truth about a relationship with the person who is dead or dying (something has died in the relationship), or it may be about what the person symbolizes in the psyche of the dreamer. The dead or dying person is then an attitude, a prejudice, or an identification or connection that is losing its influence on the dreamer.

These dreams contrast with numerous dreams I've heard about in which the person in the dream has died in reality and yet is very much alive in the dream. In these dreams, the dreamer is aware that the person has died and is glad to see him or her in the dream itself. These dreams often come when it is important to be reminded that something about that person or what he or she represents continues to be very much alive. They differ in quality and intensity from "visitation dreams," which come while the dreamer is still in mourning and has a vivid dream that has the impact of a real visit.

Interpretation of a myth or a dream, or of a synchronistic event in real life that can be interpreted as a dream, is another approach to deepening the meaning. It begins with "What if?" What if this myth fascinates you because there is "something" more to glean from it? What if the major characters are all inner figures? Who, then, is Meleager? In Jungian psychology, he is the inner masculine in a woman—the *animus*, who, in partnership with the feminine ego, faces the boar. He is the ability to act decisively, objectively, impersonally, and effectively in concert with a conscious and courageous feminine who faces her emotion-laden shadow.

When you shift the protagonist role from Atalanta to Meleager in the hunt for the boar and consider the death of Meleager as symbolic, it becomes another very meaningful story with parallels in real life. Meleager comes to the gathering of the hunters with Atalanta at his side. But this hunt is a guy-thing! She doesn't belong there! Her presence is not welcomed; there is muttering against her. Until then, the relationship between the two was a private, in-the-forest relationship—meaning that it was either closeted from others or, as a feminine aspect in his psyche, was developing in the privacy of his inner world. His bond with her is an authentic choice, not one made by collective values or family expectations. To bring Atalanta to the hunt and defend her right to be there makes their relationship public. With the objective being the hunt, and each man intent on gaining fame for himself, arguing over her presence is put aside.

Then comes the hunt itself. Atalanta draws the first blood with her arrow; Meleager strkes the decisive blow with his sword; together they bring down the boar and he gives her the trophy pelt. Outrage over the gift stirs up resentment and Meleager kills his uncles. His uncles, however, are extensions of his mother—her *animus* figures, upholders of her rights and attitudes, symbols of her power over her son's emotional life. When Meleager kills them, he is symbolically killing his mother's influence over who he loves and what he does. This causes his mother to reassert her power over her son's life, killing first him and then herself.

The energy bonds between two people that define a relationship need to be taken down *by both* for the old pattern to truly be over. As a metaphor in real life, this is about the painful separation between the hold of a mother (or father) who lives through the son (or daughter or spouse) and the life planned for him and his becoming his own person. The deaths of mother and son symbolize the end of this old bond. In real life, however, there are more chapters yet to come.

Chapter Five

ATALANTA IN THE WILDERNESS

After Meleager's death, Atalanta wanders alone in the forests of Calydon—in the wilderness, a terrain that is more familiar and safer for her than a castle. This is a time of mourning and grief. She will never be with Meleager again. A phase of her life is over and gone. She can not bring him or it back again. Atalanta is in a major transition. This is the time between what was and what is to come, a transition zone defined by time and place, by an ending.

Loss that changes your life comes in many forms: loss of job, loss of a belief, loss of your own health, loss of meaning, loss of a person who was central to your life. Whatever your loss, it is most important to realize that what is mourned and lost is also a sense of your old self. *Who am I now that I don't have the relationship or work or beliefs or geography that defined me?*

Wilderness is a metaphoric landscape; it is where you are in your life when you are in between one major phase or identity and the next. It's a time to make your own way, when you do not know what will come next or how you will change. It is a time of transition. It may be a time to trust instinct or deep curiosity. You may find an important part of yourself in this wilderness, or lose your bearings and become lost.

The wilderness phase often comes after a significant death, or when a relationship ends, or after leaving a community. Maybe it happens when the college degree that promised employment turns out not to be a ticket to the first rung of a career, or when you have lost your job, your title, or your reputation. You are in the wilderness when you have left "who" you were, and there is no turning back. When there is no definite course to take and other people may have opinions, but don't know. It may be a time to pay attention to your inner compass of intuition, as you go in the direction toward which your soul is drawn, or sense how your body-psyche responds to each next step, or let the "soft animal of your body, love what it loves" (from Mary Oliver's poem, "Wild Geese"). Paying attention, pausing as you might from time to time, as if in an unfamiliar neighborhood, moving on when something instinctual in you knows that all is well.

First Transitions

The first loss and uncertainty about *what happens next* begins at birth, when we leave the comfort of the womb for the world, struggling through the birth canal or being suddenly lifted out via Caesarian. Everything is new and most everything new is uncomfortable—our first act is often a cry of distress as we take a first breath. I remember hearing Jungian analyst Marion Woodman, who saw the connection between body and psyche, comment that how we emerge from the womb becomes the model for later transitions. With my own two children, this proved to be true. My daughter came out headfirst in a normal and on-time delivery. My son's birth was a breech delivery, feet first, more difficult—as if he were reluctant to plunge headfirst into the world and would try an entry that took more effort on everybody's part, which a breech birth certainly does. This theme was repeated at subsequent transitions in his life. I wonder about C-section babies: Do they expect to be helped out by others and not struggle through transitions? If there is a pattern that begins at birth that may be repeated in life, then recognizing the pattern is the first step in altering it if it does not serve us or appreciating it if it makes the passage from one stage to the next easier. This is true of all significant patterns we may unconsciously repeat.

Something to ponder: What is your usual response to unwanted loss or unexpected change? When you find yourself in a transition zone, how do you react? The specific details or landscape of this new wilderness may differ, but how you respond—how you think, feel, and cope in the midst of it—may be the same. And dysfunctionally so, if you have not learned from past experience. There is a famous quote from philosopher George Santayana: "Those who cannot remember the past are condemned to repeat it" (*Reason in Common Sense*). While he was commenting on history, this clearly applies to how we live our lives as well.

TURNING TO NATURE

Shortly after she is born, Atalanta is abandoned and left to die in the wilderness. She is under the protection of

Artemis, however, who sees to it that a mother bear comes along at the crucial moment. She survives abandonment and exposure because the mother bear finds her, suckles her, and raises her like a cub. Thus from the beginning, the wilderness is kinder to Atalanta than the castle where she was born. After Meleager's death, Atalanta returns to the forest wilderness, to nature, which has proven more trustworthy than her experience with people.

Wandering through this landscape by herself, Atalanta can do the emotional work of mourning and healing from her loss of Meleager. Nature is a good place for her to do this inner work—perhaps not for every woman, but for those with Artemis as an active archetype. Out in nature, examples abound about life and death, about cycles and seasons. Everything becomes compost. Nature has a vastness about it; a human being is small next to big trees and mountains. Living in the wilderness means being under the sky during the day and the starlit heavens at night. Outdoors, proportion affects us and shows us that our particular loss is not the center of the universe. When a grieving person starts to notice beauty, which can be seen all around in nature, and hears the song of birds and the sound of water, or enjoys the light and warmth of the sun, then healing has begun. Trees help. There is solace in sitting in the shade of a tree, listening to the wind through its leaves, or putting your arms around its trunk or your cheek against its bark.

To navigate alone through grief and mourning is common when society's values assume that you have no right to grieve at all. Or that it is a weakness. Or is offensive to someone who can't tolerate either grief or grief for this particular loss. If you are under the protection of Artemis and the one-in-yourself virgin goddess archetypes, you have inner support to be yourself, but in private. The wilderness into which you can retreat will be with nature, or into your inner world. Without this protection, especially in childhood—you are likely to accept the judgments of others that your reaction is bad or that you are bad, or don't have the right to feel the way you do. The seeds of feeling something is wrong with you are planted or fertilized by this. (Boys raised in patriarchy learn to suppress grief by transforming it into anger, blame, or getting even someday unless they have a strong connection to this same goddess in themselves). Go into your own wilderness to express the love and the loss through something you do or create, through words in a journal, art, ritual, or poetry, or go into nature to build a cairn or labyrinth out of stones; make sacred spaces on beaches, under trees, on hilltops or mountains. This is what Artemis people do in the wilderness of loss. Which, as I think of the image of Artemis with her dog and those I have known who grieved for animals, is how in privacy and in nature they grieved for a beloved animal instead of feeling ashamed—which others feel who have internalized the view that "It's only a dog!" (Marohn, *What The Animals Taught Me*).

STRAYED

Real people whose lives become engrossing tales can be seen as mythic role models themselves when they touch on archetypal imagery or themes. This certainly is true for Cheryl Strayed, author of *Wild: From Lost to Found on the*

Pacific Crest Trail (2012). Cheryl wrote about the thousand-mile, three-month trek she took on her own—an idea/impulse/determination/calling/compulsion that she followed. I feel that she enacted the spirit in the poem "Artemis" by Olga Broumas:

> *I am a woman*
> *who understands*
> *the necessity of an impulse whose goal or origin*
> *still lie beyond me.*

The "necessity of an impulse" is what Stayed heeded. She remembered hearing of the Pacific Crest Trail and was intrigued when it came up again. There were no logical reasons for her being so drawn to it, much less for her walking it by herself. It was beyond her to know why, but within her there was this compelling necessity.

It's true that we define ourselves through our decisions and actions. Cheryl took defining herself one step further when she chose a name for herself. "Strayed" is not her real name, and she never tells her readers the name that she was born with in her book. When she was contemplating divorce, she realized that she could not continue using the hyphenated married name that she shared with her husband, nor could she go back to using the name she had before, any more than she could be the girl she used to be. She tried on many last names that sounded good with Cheryl. Nothing fit until the word "strayed" came to mind. She looked up the meaning in the dictionary and *knew* it was hers: "to wander from the proper path, to deviate from the direct course, to be lost, to become wild, to be without a mother or father, to be without a home, to move about aimlessly in search of something, to diverge or digress."

By emphasizing that Cheryl was following an inner knowing, I am bringing up once again what I have said in many of my previous books, because this is crucial to living an authentic life—one that is your own and not a map you are expected to follow. To recognize *gnosis,* which is intuitively felt knowledge, is to *know* what feels true for you. Then comes the next significant question: Will you follow where it leads?

For Cheryl Strayed, the recent death of her mother, the long-past death of her father, the end of her marriage, and bad decisions made in the aftermath were precursors to her decision to follow her inner knowing. The trek she embarked on took her from the Mojave Desert to the Cascades and into meditative reflections on her life, calling upon perseverance and heart when the going was rough and finding grace and gratitude for what she experienced and found in herself. I imagine that when Cheryl decided to write a book, what she learned through walking the Pacific Crest Trail carried over into her writing. Both were decisions that grew out of a belief that this—the trek, then the book—was important to do. Then came the commitment to do it. She stuck with that commitment as she took one step at a time, one page at a time, until so many miles and pages later, she had done what she set out to do. And I suspect that, in the doing, she found herself fully absorbed in the present moment—and, on the trail, fully in her body as well. It is soul-nourishing to do whatever it is that gives you this experience.

The wilderness is beautiful—nature is. Whether actually or metaphorically, there is beauty and timelessness to be found in the wilderness, and *in yourself* when you leave your usual life behind and follow the impulse that leads you to do what you love and be where you want to be. Doing something that is really hard is satisfying.

Under the Protection of Artemis

Women who feel a strong necessity or impulse to spend time in nature, those who take up a physical outdoor challenge, have a connection with the Artemis archetype. I think of Elizabeth Danu's decision to take a long bike trip on her own—from Seattle to San Diego, a journey of six weeks that covered over 1,600 miles (*www.theliberationofpersephone.com*). Like Cheryl Strayed, Elizabeth was not adequately prepared. She had never biked carrying sixty pounds with her, and her legs were just not used to it. On day four, biking against headwinds, her legs not only hurt so badly that she wanted to stop, they were shaking uncontrollably. She had covered only half the miles to the campground that was the goal for this day. She stopped by the side of the road and considered her options. Should she bail and not go on with the whole thing? She was half way to the campground, so going back the way she came would take the same amount of effort as going forward. This was something she had determined to do—it was important to no one else. This was a moment of truth. With no one else involved, Elizabeth told herself: "You decided to do this!" She got back on the bike, her legs still shaking from fatigue. It seemed miraculous, but the wind died down as soon as she resumed.

Elizabeth made it to the campground after dark, only to learn that every space had been taken. Before she had to figure what her next move would be, someone called to her that there was ample space where they were camped—and they fed her well to boot. After day four, when her resolve had been tested, she found that, instead of battling headwinds, she had "wind under her wings"—one of my favorite expressions. It was as if grace accompanied her the rest of the way. This was especially true thirty miles north of Monterey, when she discovered that a bridge her guidebook told her to take was out, with no alternative route given. As she pondered what to do, she tells us, "five guys on bikes pulled up. It could have been very bad, but as it turned out they were born-again Christians from Whittier, California. They had a map and invited me to ride with them." Ten minutes after she joined them, her last tire blew and they had a spare.

Synchronicity and Grace

Elizabeth on her bike trip and Cheryl on the Pacific Crest Trail describe unexpected help that came their way, which I see as *synchronistic* events. "Synchronicity" is a word coined by Jung to describe meaningful coincidences that occur between the inner world and outer events. Whenever this happens, I feel blessed by grace and feel gratitude for it. This was the subject of my first book, *The Tao of Psychology: Synchronicity and the Self* (1999), which supports the experience of people whose actions and intentions are motivated by a connection to the Self (archetype of meaning, divinity, the Tao, God/Goddess, higher power) and who find that they get "help from the universe." This has been my experience, and also something I see happening to others when ego-Self and archetype are aligned. Both Cheryl and Elizabeth heeded an inner directive from the Artemis archetype and received frequent, unexpected, synchronistic help along their way. It can be said that they were "under Artemis' protection"—just as it was said of the infant Atalanta when she was saved by a mother bear.

Like Cheryl Strayed, Elizabeh Danu also chose her own last name. "Danu" is the Celtic mother/warrior goddess. "By choosing that name at thirty-three, I declared that I am a daughter of the Goddess. My own last name didn't seem relevant to me anymore. It was my Dad's name given to him by his stepfather, paternal generation after generation."

It took grit, a combination of perseverance and passion, for both women to follow a strong impulsive decision and stick to it. From the beginning, they had to resist advice from concerned and well-meaning people against following their impulses. They had time to fulfill their commitment to themselves because they were both in a time of transition. When the journeys they undertook were over, both had been changed by doing what they set out to do; both had found strength and a belief in themselves as a result.

Years later, when she was forty-five, Elizabeth developed inflammatory breast cancer (IFC stage 3C), which is a particularly malignant form of the disease that has to be treated aggressively. In this crisis, she drew on the same proven grit that had gotten her back on her bike—this time in order to go through the chemotherapy that wiped her out with each treatment. Her children were seven and nine at the time; she had been through a "horrific" divorce. She was determined to raise her children; to do this, it was imperative that she live. She was *not* going to leave the planet! This meant to her that she would not miss a single chemo treatment, no matter what. To help her get through this, the bike trip became her own mythic story. She has since passed the five-year marker. Still cancer-free in 2014, she created a resource website for cancer survivors—The Liberation of Persephone (*www.theliberationofpersephone.com*).

The abduction of Persephone is one of the most familiar Greek myths, one with which everyone—men as well as women—can identify once the analogy hits home. Persephone is gathering flowers in a meadow when the earth opens and, out of the deep dark chasm, Hades comes to abduct her into the underworld. One day, everything is as usual, and then . . . the underworld—you get a cancer diagnosis; you are fired; your child is missing; you have been left or betrayed by someone you counted on. Suddenly, you find yourself in a world full of uncertainties, fears, and possibilities—and this new terrain is a wilderness.

Atalanta begins her life in the wilderness; after Meleager's death, she finds herself alone in another kind of wildness. Just as she is rejected and abandoned at the beginning of her life for being a girl, she is rejected as unsuitable for Meleager by his mother and, regardless of her ability and courage as a hunter, is rejected as a female by the other hunters.

Atalanta's story resonates with women—especially those from past generations who, like her, excelled in accomplishments but, instead of being rewarded with the trophy and cheered, had it snatched away just as Meleager's uncles tried to do with the pelt. Many learned firsthand that rules are changed when "the wrong type" or "wrong gender" person qualifies to win the prize. Awards that should go to the student with the best grades or the one who does the best work go to someone else "more appropriate" to represent the school or the town. At least this was true before the empowerment of members of a wronged group made such actions indefensible or politically incorrect, before justice or fairness became the standard.

There are plenty of women who remember times when they deserved an honor or recognition that went to someone else. They were expected to be good sports or be understanding. Candace Pert, the immunologist whose discovery of opiate receptors was critical to the success of the research, was left off the all-male team of investigators nominated for the Albert Lasker Award that leads to the Nobel Prize. Likewise, Rosalind Franklin, the woman scientist who should have been credited with discovering the molecular structure of DNA and the double-helix structure of the chromosome, never received recognition for her work. James Watson, Francis Crick, and Maurice Wilkins published their work, which was based on her discovery, and received the Nobel Prize in physiology (1953). Franklin died from cancer five years later. Pert, knowing of the relationship between depression and a depressed immune system that can lead to the development of cancer, drew a lesson from Franklin's experience that led her to speak out, instead of being "a good sport or team player," which she was urged to do.

Candace Pert protested rather than remain silent, which is what a woman with a strong Artemis archetype would do. She sent a letter to the head of the foundation that awards the Lasker Award describing her contribution to the discovery (she had not even been cited in the submission). That she dared to do so caused a sensation in the field. The 1979 award nonetheless went to Solomon H. Snyder, who headed the lab. Snyder did laud her in his acceptance speech, however, and did not go on to win the Nobel Prize, both consequences of her action. He was also quoted as saying: "That's how the game is played." And he went on to say that, when she became head of her own lab, Pert would do the same (Schwartz, *New York Times*, 2013). Instead, following her Artemis archetype, Pert went into new areas of research in neuroscience, immunology, and mind-body concepts. She set her sights on research targets of her own choosing—to make discoveries in "wilderness" areas of knowledge—and went on a hunt for scientific evidence for what she intuitively knew.

Betrayal by Brothers in Arms

Women who respond to the invitation to join the armed forces heed a call to adventure. They are promised the opportunity to travel and to be part of a team, to serve their country and receive training and education, and to get away from the limitations of their normal lives, if only they have the courage and grit to do so. Just like Atalanta, who would have joined up as an Argonaut—which Robert Graves says she did in his version of *The Golden Fleece* (2003). A woman who joins up to fight often has had very positive experiences with brothers or with male friends. Because of this, if a man (or men) with whom she serves sexually assaults her and others stand by and don't intervene, she is not only raped, but also betrayed. She experiences a loss of trust and innocence. When she is violated, demeaned, and dirtied by the not-uncommon reality of rape in the military, she feels isolated and wary of the men with whom she serves, rather than feeling that she is able to count on them.

Women in the military are taught to believe in the military code of loyalty and trust. They thus suffer a profound sense of trauma and betrayal when they are sexually assaulted by a fellow soldier. That sense of betrayal deepens when they report this to superior officers and then are retaliated against and discharged under false claims that they have mental disorders. Investigative reporting in 2013 by the *San Antonio Express-News* into the pervasive and long-standing problem of sexual assaults in the military substantiate this. In the Annual Department of Defense Report (2012), there were 3,374 reported cases of sexual assault in the military and only 238 convictions. Indeed, the Pentagon's anonymous survey of members of the military led it to estimate that more than 26,000 women and men had been sexually assaulted. More may have been reported, in part due to the 2012 release of the Academy Award-nominated documentary film, *The Invisible War,* written and directed by Kirby Dick. Kirsten Gillibrand, junior senator from New York, watched this film at home, and then saw it again with her staff and decided to make the issue of sexual abuse in the military a priority. She proposed what was considered a radical solution—to have military prosecutors rather than commanding officers decide which sexual assault cases would be tried.

What if, at the end of the hunt, Meleager had not stood by Atalanta? The trophy would have been snatched away, and worse might have happened. With the adrenaline and testosterone running high among the hunters, the ego blow of being bested by a woman at a male game, resentment at her, and the need to exert their power—remember, the king had characterized these men as men who took what they wanted—a gang rape might have resulted.

This happens in the armed services and whenever bullying and rape occur with no Meleager in the crowd. Perpetrators rape and bully, while other men participate in the act by watching and not doing anything to stop it.

The hunt for the boar bears an emotional and physical resemblance to the experience of troops in Iraq and Afghanistan as they hunt for insurgents and the Taliban. The boar is initially hidden from the hunters behind dense cover. It suddenly emerges and charges them, trampling, goring, and throwing those nearest over its horns as others get out of its way or use their weapons ineffectively. The hunters are thus like soldiers who are splattered by blood and even body parts when their buddies take hits from improvised explosive devices. An awful experience—yet spared and still in danger. This makes both hunters and soldiers grasp their weapons more tightly and puts them on heightened alert. They are adrenalized for flight or fight, yet must not run away and be marked as cowards. When the perpetrators are hidden or disappear into the crowd (or the wilderness), there is no enemy to confront, no one appropriate upon whom to discharge their fear and aggression. This can lead to impotence and frustration that can be taken out on women. When soldiers in combat are wounded or killed by their own forces, we make the assumption that these are tragic accidents, that they are casualties of "friendly fire." Not so when a woman is raped by a fellow soldier, and then betrayed by the military hierarchy when she reports it.

Wilderness As Metaphor

The loss of a significant relationship through death, estrangement, rejection, or betrayal—or loss of a position, financial security, or reputation; or of trust, innocence, or faith; or of health that creates a risk of dying—can take the person who suffers the loss into a psychological wilderness or underworld where there are no longer defined paths to walk or landmarks to follow. In *Close to the Bone: Life-Threatening Illness as a Soul Journey* (2007), I describe the inner experience of a cancer diagnosis as an abduction or descent into the underworld, with parallels to Persephone's abduction or Inanna's descent in their respective myths. There is ordinary life before the diagnosis and a very different world after it. What was important before is no longer so, and you find yourself for a time not knowing what to do or which direction to take. In either the metaphoric wilderness or the underworld, there is a loss of your usual bearings and a need for reorientation to a new and scary time and place. You are at a crossroad, and what you do matters.

The loss of a significant relationship—spouse, lover, child, parent, mentor, or friend; the loss of your home; or the loss of a position or role—often ends a phase of life and begins a period of personal crisis. Symbols for "danger" and "opportunity" are the two elements that, together, comprise the Chinese pictograph for "crisis." In the birth process, the transition stage is the most dangerous to the life of the mother and the baby. This occurs when the head of the baby goes under the pubic bone of the mother; it is the last stage before birth. Transition and crisis do go together—with new life a possibility if you move through this phase successfully and do not give up on yourself or on life.

To find yourself psychologically in a metaphoric wilderness or underworld is to cross into your own interior world—a world that may contain painful memories you have put aside and feelings you have suppressed. When bad things happen to you—like Meleager dying at the height of Atalanta's accomplishments—there is a danger of seeing yourself as a victim, of becoming depressed and stuck, or full of blame and rage. Better to explore this new terrain, to see what is there, than to give up. In the metaphoric wilderness, there are vast unexplored regions. In the underworld, there are buried riches. These are your own undeveloped talents and archetypes, qualities that were not approved of or valued by others that can become sources of meaning. The good and bad, gold and dross, that are found can contribute to the next stage of your life, enabling you to become more of who you really are and can be.

If, like Atalanta, you are on your own and have past experience and survival skills to call on—psychological and spiritual, as well as practical, knowledge—you may experience hardship and loneliness, but trust that this is part of your soul path that gives it meaning. And this makes all the difference. When you are in the midst of a wilderness or a dark wood and trust that this is terrain you must go through, it will have meaning. It may feel like a maze full of dead ends, but it will turn out to be a labyrinthine path full of U-turns. "This, too, shall pass." This Sufi saying, at the darkest moments, helps you endure painful uncertainty without giving in to fear and hopelessness. It echoes the wisdom of the ancient Chinese *Book of Changes* known as the *I Ching,* which observes that change is the only certainty. To be discerning about what to do next and maintain hope are essential. Vaclav Havel, poet and playwright, and first president of a free Czechoslovakia after the oppressive Soviet occupation, expressed it thus in his book *Disturbing the Peace* (1986):

> *Hope is an orientation of spirit; hope is an orientation of the heart. It is not the certainty that something will turn out well but the conviction that something makes sense no matter how it turns out.*

Moving Through the Wilderness

Most women who identify with the Artemis archetype are not susceptible to prolonged wanderings in the wilderness of depression or obsessions brought on by deep personal loss. This archetype predisposes people to independence and autonomy, which lessens the impact of the loss of a person, unlike the archetypes that are fulfilled through being a mother (Demeter) or a wife (Hera). For these archetypes, the loss of a relationship, the loss of a role, and the loss of meaning compound the personal loss and can make it psychologically disabling.

The ability to get over a loss and move on seems to be an archetypal characteristic, yet this can be misleading—like camouflage—for it would be just like an Atalanta/Artemis woman to hide her grief from the view of others instinctively. However, Artemis women don't usually get stuck in or become passive captives in the underworld; this is a Persephone journey. Demeter's response to loss is to become seriously depressed; Hera's reaction is to avoid knowing how bad she feels and instead to blame and seek revenge on others. These are patterns that can take possession of women who lose someone important to them through death, infidelity, or estrangement. An emotional abduction into a cult or by a controlling person is a Persephone story.

Atalanta's time in the wilderness is not accounted for in Greek mythology. Meleager dies at the end of the hunt; at some indeterminate time later, Atalanta turns up in Arcadia where she was born. To get from the forests of Calydon to Arcadia to meet the father who rejected her at birth, she has to travel the distance on foot through the forests that covered most of Greece. This would have been a journey through a real wilderness measured in miles, some of which may also have been spent in grief or anger—out of sight of anyone.

The Wilderness of Possibility and Potential

Once you are on your own, once you can't return to who you were and who you were with, once you are in a new landscape—in a place and among people who are new to you, and you new to them—then who you used to be no longer defines you. There is no beaten path or broad well-traveled road to follow. In this new wilderness of mind and reality, if you follow your own instincts—which may be a strong impulse, intuition, or curiosity—you can make a path where there is no path, one that becomes truly your own.

In our lives, two forces shape who we become: outer expectations that are conventional and often limiting that we succeed (or not) at meeting, and traits of character and instinct that are ingrained or archetypal. When circumstances—what happens *to* you—bring you into uncharted terrain, what is *in* you is tested. Once you are in the wilderness, there are questions whose answers you can only find through living the experience. How will you respond? Are you resilient? Will you have the courage to follow what feels true or right for you? Will you be able to say "no" to what others would have you do or be? Can you wait until you become clear about what you will do next? Will you trust that you will recognize a whole-hearted "yes"?

Meanwhile, when you are on your own in a wilderness phase, the decisions you make are often about the small steps. Yet each one is significant, an opportunity to practice discernment. Which is the next *right* step? When you awake to find yourself in a dark wood—what will you do next?

In my forty-ninth year, I found myself echoing Dante's words: "In the mid-point of my life, I awoke to find myself in a dark wood." I had left a twenty-year marriage and was now in my own wilderness, wondering: What next? The answer arrived in the mail—an invitation to visit sacred sites in Europe. In timing and meaning, this was a remarkable synchronicity. My acceptance of the invitation was an initiation into pilgrimage, which deepened my spiritual intuition and led me to write *Crossing to Avalon: A Woman's Midlife Pilgrimage* (1994), now subtitled *A Woman's Search for the Sacred Feminine*. This was a next step on my soul path.

To travel while paying attention to your dreams, memories, synchronicities, sensations, and images can make any journey an inner pilgrimage to sources of meaning. Spending time in the wilderness of nature is a pilgrimage to the sacred feminine for many Atalanta/Artemis women, especially those who journal each day, taking the time to write and reflect upon the journey. Travel is an attractive and intriguing option for Artemis women who are in a transition and have the means to set off on an adventure that is also a journey of self-discovery. This was true for Elizabeth Gilbert, who wrote *Eat, Pray, Love: One Woman's Search for Everything Across Italy, India, and Indonesia* (2006).

Another metaphoric wilderness resides in your own creativity, where thoughts, feelings, and images are stirred into new forms or expressed in new ways, which can lead to discoveries and creative works. Any artist, writer, musician, creative thinker, or researcher whose creative process takes him or her into virgin territory is in this wilderness. This often requries moving away from institutions and the usual crowd of like-minded people—whether therapists, artists, or academicians—to find different eyes with which to see. Georgia O'Keeffe is an example of an artist whose distinctive style emerged after she experienced and incorporated the effects of living for a time on the Great Plains of the United States. After one visit to New Mexico, she recognized that this was the landscape that most evoked and inspired her; so this was where she moved after her husband, Alfred Stieglitz, died. To Artemis, the land of the soul is in the natural world.

Atalanta has to make her way there through a forested terrain where there are no paths other than animal tracks, where obstacles like steep ravines or rivers challenge her. She has to forage or hunt for food, and find shelter at night. She travels light and stays only briefly in any one place. This is not unlike the situation for women who no longer have the work, school, or relationship that previously defined their lives and may now have financial concerns as well. Temporary shelter with parents, relatives, or friends—shared housing—may be necessary, especially when there is unemployment and a recession economy.

Atalanta comes to the decision to return to Arcadia where she was born, not knowing how she will be received. This takes courage of a different kind than that required to face the boar. While she can count on her physical courage and her skill as a hunter, she feels no certainty about being welcomed home. That is a decision made by the heart, with hope that there will be a place for her now that she has proven herself. This is a hope held by daughters who have been rejected by their fathers who then go into the world and excel. They hope that their accomplishments will make their fathers proud of them. Under this hope lies the bigger hope that their fathers will love them. Wanting this while knowing that it may not be exposes their vulnerability, which is an act of courage. It's the same for the young woman who is adopted and later in life seeks her birth mother. Likewise for the mother who gave up her baby for adoption and then seeks to meet her child as an adult. It takes courage to love someone who may not reciprocate, to want to be loved or want to be forgiven. And while this requires courage of a different kind, courage is like a muscle that grows with exercise. Moreover, courage in one part of our lives does carry over to other parts.

However it turns out, the "return home"—seeking to find a birth mother or a child given up for adoption, or seeking out people who were once very important with whom connection was severed or lost, especially when you did the leaving (which is typically Artemis)—is a reunion fraught with the possibility of rejection and anger, or of seeing consequences for which you may have been responsible, at least in part. Yet this return is also potentially healing and revealing, even or especially so when it is your shadow that is revealed to you. Then you may receive unsought lessons in humility or grow in compassion for yourself and others. The timing and the decision for doing this often arise during a time of transition. Moving on psychologically may require returning to past relationships, which can be done in person, as Atalanta sets out to do. However, returning home psychologically is the work of psychotherapy and analysis, which, for many people, means finding their own inner abandoned child.

Chapter Six

The Footrace and the Three Golden Apples

The fame of Atalanta precedes her to Arcadia and to her father. Years have passed and he has not had the son and heir he desires, so, when he realizes that Atalanta is the daughter he ordered abandoned, he acknowledges her as his daughter.

In the contemporary world, Atalanta represents the once-ignored daughter who succeeds and has grown into a person in her own right. Perhaps a son or son-surrogates did not turn out to have the competence or ambition expected by the father; or perhaps a father—wary, as in real and mythic stories, of sons who may depose or supplant him—now undertakes to mentor a daughter to take up the duties, expectations, and responsibilities of heir apparent.

In the myth, Atalanta herself becomes a prize to be acquired. She is beautiful, famous, and heir to a kingdom. When she inherits the throne, her husband will be king. Suitors come, but she is not interested. Once she is recognized by her father, however, she comes under his dominion again. Just as he could order that she be disposed of at birth, now he can demand that she marry. She is no longer a free, adventuresome, capable, and independent woman with goals of her own. She no longer has sovereignty over herself; she belongs to her father until she marries. Then she will belong to her husband.

FLEET-FOOTED ATALANTA

Atalanta is famous as a runner as well as a hunter. Women runners are a common sight today—for many, a daily run is part of their routine. Running fits as an Artemis activity, because it is something a woman can do by herself that takes her out of the house or away from work and into the outdoors—on trails or through parks, and as close to nature as can be fit into the day. There is something very one-in-yourself about being a runner. You do it because you want to and because it pleases you. If you decide to run a certain distance and improve your time, this is a target of your own choosing. If you decide to enter a race, the most common reason to do so is to achieve a personal goal. Running makes you feel competent; you have sovereignty over yourself while you run; you can clear your mind and be in the present moment. Fleet-footed runners can also get into the "zone" associated with endorphins—a "runner's high."

Women enter races of varying lengths, from sprints to marathons. Many are benefits to raise money for good causes. Run for the Cure, which benefits breast cancer research, is a well-organized and well-known example, in which women recruit friends and relatives to sponsor their efforts. Each sponsor agrees to donate a certain amount per mile the runner runs. This principle can be used for any cause by runners who want to inform people about a cause or a need, and to raise money for it. I learned about how this works when Heather C. Brewer, a college woman in North Carolina, initiated a run to raise money for Earth Child Institute after learning about what this organization does in my book *Like a Tree* (2011).

Another run, this one for Women in the Congo, was the inspiration of Lisa Shannon, who, after watching the *Oprah* show one afternoon, was appalled to learn about "the war people don't know about." She heard from journalist Lisa Ling about the violence in the Congo that had killed four million people and about the rape atrocities and sexual slavery routinely inflicted on women. Zainab Salbi, founder of Women to Women International, the organization that is helping Congolese women heal and become empowered, showed a video of these women. Their faces stayed with Lisa. Women to Women International is an amazing and effective organization that provides a way for women to sponsor women who have become the collateral damage of conflicts in the world. She said that a Congolese woman could be sponsored for twenty-seven dollars a month. Lisa decided that she would do this. When she found herself on the verge of being distracted from her commitment, she caught herself, saying: "I have to do it now, before it becomes one more thing I *meant* to do." Then she immediately went to her computer to sign up to sponsor two women (one of 6,000 *Oprah* viewers who did this).

The feeling that she needed to do more kept coming back in Lisa's mind. She tried to convince her friends to join her in creating a 5K walk or run for women in the Congo, but none of them agreed or cared to learn about the conflict. She knew she had to do something to convince her friends and family how serious, how personal, this was to her. She decided to run the entire length of the rugged Wildwood Forest trail through Portland's West Hills. Her goal was to raise thirty-one sponsorships—one for each mile. She kept her intention a secret initially, because she was not sure she could do it. She had been a casual runner.

It took four months of serious training to prepare for the run. Every day, she hit the trail alone; each week, she went on the longest run of her life. Her mother pitched *The Oregonian* to do a feature article on her run; friends hosted events where she showed clips from *Oprah* and talked about why she was doing her run. Her dedication was convincing. On the big day, she ran the whole 31.16 miles and raised $28,000, which sponsored eighty Congolese women. Her Run for Congo Women was grassroots activism—something she was moved to do to help the women in the Congo. And it led to doing more. It took her to the Congo to meet the women she was sponsoring, and motivated her to write *A Thousand Sisters: My Journey into the Worst Place on Earth to be a Woman* (2010). One right step led to the next right step, and then to the next—which is how most heart-centered activists find that they are on a soul path.

That there are women runners hardly seems remarkable in this day and age, yet it took consciousness-raising and women acting together to make this so. In 1972, six women entered the New York City Marathon, challenging the American Athletic Union rule that barred women. The AAU justified their ban with unfounded "scientific" research, including claims that women who ran more than a few miles risked infertility. The organizer of the marathon courted women runners and got the AAU to relent somewhat: "certain women" could take part provided that they started ten minutes before or after the men on a different starting line. An article in *Runner's World* (Robinson, October 2012) described the scene. Six women lined up at the starting line for their ten-minute head start. The women spread across the line side by side, the gun went off, and the women sat down and held up signs mocking the AAU. The photo ran across four columns of the Monday *New York Times* and that helped to launch a running revolution for women.

Nina Kuscsik, onc of the six, made running history in 1972 when she became the first woman to win the Boston Marathon. Another lasting image of a pioneering runner was taken just five years previous to that, in 1967 in Boston. The photo shows the enraged director of the Boston Marathon attacking Kathrine Switzer as she is midstride on the marathon course. He tries to take her bib/number off and is thwarted by a body block by her boyfriend (another man in the role of Meleager). At a time when women were banned from the race, Switzer became the first woman to finish the course, wearing an unofficial bib number on her shirt.

"How dare she!" anger is directed at women who do not do what they are told or stay in their places. Patriarchy and patriarchal men (thank goodness there are increasing numbers of men who are not) treat women as children who are supposed to obey, as possessions that belong to them, or as inferiors who deserve less of whatever is important. When women behave as if they are equal and are empowered to decide what they will do, including breaking discriminatory rules, the patriarchal response is: "How dare she!"

Changing Assumptions and Agreements

Once Atalanta is acknowledged (and legitimatized) by her father, he expects her to carry out her obligations as daughter, the first of which is to marry. In the myth, however, Atalanta negotiates conditions. The man she marries has to beat her in a footrace. And if an aspirant loses the race, he loses his life. This condition discourages some fortune hunters, and is a challenge for others who think well of themselves as winners—and probably have little or no experience losing to a girl. Atalanta's reputation in classical Greek mythology as the fleetest-footed mortal has not yet been established, but it will be through these races.

One man after another competes, and one after another loses the race. As metaphor, men who compete with women and underestimate them simply because they are women, or who overestimate their own ability and feel they are naturally superior, do lose more than one race when they lose to a woman. They feel humiliated. When men respect the women who compete with them, it is a different story.

Initially, the footraces engage Atalanta. She is fully involved in winning. Then, as one man after another races her, and one man after another loses the race and his life, it becomes routine to her. She knows she is really good at running and the races offer no real challenge. So it can be for women who enter the competitive world of men and become really good at what they do. The Atalanta/Artemis in them gets bored at winning, once they master the skill involved or there is no new terrain to explore. Mere winning for the sake of winning, or for the acquisition of power and money, are not major motivations for an Artemis. Nor is she interested in suitors who are drawn to her persona and who see her as a prize. The beauty, fame, and possessions that make Atalantas attractive to men are superficial attributes to those women themselves.

HIPPOMENES AND THE FOOTRACE

Finally, there is only one suitor left—Hippomenes. All of the rest sought to beat Atalanta to acquire a trophy wife and a kingdom. Hippomenes, on the other hand, sees her race, fearing each time that another man may win and have her. He knows that she can beat him; yet, because he loves her, he puts his life on the line and enters the race. He may know of her grief at the death of Meleager and of how she left Calydon, where there are only painful memories for her.

The night before the race, Hippomenes prays to Aphrodite, Goddess of Love and Beauty, that Atalanta might love him and that he might win her. All of the other suitors also prayed before they raced, but they prayed to Hermes or Zeus or Ares for speed or power in order that they might defeat Atalanta. Aphrodite hears in Hippomenes' prayers the wish to win her for *love* and, when he wakes in the morning, he sees three gleaming golden apples left by the goddess.

Atalanta waits at the starting line for this last race to begin. She takes no pleasure in the prospect of defeating Hippomenes, which is, for her, a foregone conclusion. As he approaches, she notices that he is holding his hands over the band in his tunic (where the three golden apples are hidden), which she finds peculiar. This reminds her of how Meleager suddenly put his hands in a similar position just before he died. She has put this horrible moment out of her mind and, with it, the memories of the closeness and idyllic times she had with him.

The Artemis/Atalanta woman can often put aside memories of the past to focus on something current that absorbs her interest. Long-distance runners push themselves and their bodies to reach new goals and don't look back as they do. Yet looking back, remembering and reflecting upon past experiences, is the inner task at hand for women with this archetype. Until midlife or mid-career, especially if they are outer-directed, they have lived out aspects of Artemis as goddess of the hunt. When they are able to stop running and lose interest in winning, there comes a time when they can turn to Artemis as goddess of the moon. This draws them inward—to reflect upon the past, to attend to dreams, and to see shades of gray in the behavior and motivation of self and others. They no longer judge people and circumstances simply in terms of black or white, good or bad, right or wrong. With reflection, they can see that patterns and compassion can enter in.

Atalanta, being reminded of Meleager's death, loses her focus just as the signal is given to begin the race. Hippomenes immediately takes off down the track; Atalanta is distracted long enough to give him a good head start. When she realizes that the race has begun and Hippomenes is out in front, she comes back to her usual competitive self and, because she excels at this, it takes her very little time to catch up. In no time, she is at his heels. A few more strides and she will pass him—except that she doesn't. At that moment, Hippomenes tosses a golden apple into her path. It is just too beautiful, especially in the glow of sunlight, to pass up. Atalanta slows down to pick it up, and Hippomenes spurts ahead.

At this point in the race, we know that there are two more golden apples to come. What do they represent? What appears in an Atalanta/Artemis woman's life to distract her, to draw her inward so she can react to other stirrings in her psyche?

The First Apple: Awareness of Time Passing

Atalanta is drawn to the shining beauty of the first golden apple. She picks it up, gazes at it, and can see her face mirrored back, distorted by the curves of the apple. The thought enters her mind: This is how I will look when I grow old.

Women who are focused on what they are doing, who set long-term goals for themselves, and for whom accomplishments or mastery of something are all-absorbing often do not pay much attention to the passing of time. They don't chart the effects of time on their faces. Women for whom being attractive to men is essential notice the beginning of aging with a slight sag or a wrinkle years before an Artemis/Atalanta notices that she is slowing down, or that she is not as keen about challenges or reaching goals, or that her fascination with exploration and new horizons is waning. Atalanta's thought that the apple shows her how she will look when she grows old brings with it an insight that may never have occurred to her before: *I* shall grow old someday.

The insight here is the awareness of time passing. This may occur at any age in adulthood, especially when there are markers to meet—the "by now you should have . . ." expectations. In the mid-thirties to mid-forties, the idea of midlife arises when you realize that the decades have passed quickly. The time you have left may equal the years that have passed so far—and how quickly those years went by! As people live longer and healthier lives, vitality extends life and the quality of it. Active, engaged-in-life women of sixty, seventy, or even eighty may pause and give thought to time passing when they realize that they are within sight of the finish line. Reaching the chronological age at which a parent died often causes us to pause on the track and reflect, perhaps more objectively than before because we are now of the same age. Thoughts about time passing may also bring up the realization that death may come at any age; it's not only an octogenarian who should have documents, wishes, and finances in order and be current with the people who matter, especially when it comes to speaking from the heart.

The Second Apple: Awareness of the Importance of Love

When Atalanta slows down to pick up the first golden apple and pauses to gaze at it, Hippomenes races ahead. As soon as she realizes this, she refocuses on the race and effortlessly gains on him. She would pass him, except that he throws another golden apple in her path, which rolls away onto the side of the track. She retrieves it, giving Hippomenes time to increase his lead.

The second golden apple stirs in Atalanta a yearning for the physical and emotional closeness she once had with Meleager. The painful memory brought back by Hippomenes' clutching his belt also brings back the good times she spent with Meleager and their beautiful shared experiences. While it is common to want to avoid thinking about a relationship that ended painfully, when the loved moments are remembered as well, an important question arises: Would it have been better not to have loved at all?

Atalanta begins life learning to count on nature and animals for solace; people are not there for her. She more or less raises herself. By virtue of archetype and circumstance, she learns to be self-sufficient. She is one-in-herself as a child; she does not count on others. Perhaps she has imaginary playmates as well as animals and birds as friends.

Meleager overcomes her mistrust and becomes her companion and defender. He admires her competency and sees her as beautiful. He is her male counterpart, and perhaps her lover—even if, as is likely, she did not fall in love with him as he did with her. They explore and hunt together. He is her first best friend—until his mother breaks up the relationship, kills him off, and leaves her with the pain and loss. But when you remember fully and know that a relationship is significant and soul-growing, no matter how it ends, it can lead you to gratitude for having had the experience and the person. And no matter how long the relationship lasts, you can also come to have gratitude for the grief that goes with loss. It may seem strange to be glad to grieve, but if you learned that there was no sympathy for tears or sadness, and had an innate strength of will and ability to focus, grief is held in and tears are held back. When these feelings finally well up and you sob with deep grief, it opens a channel to your feelings, which become more accessible to you and make it possible to open your heart more to others.

Aphrodite stirs yearnings in us for love and creates the attraction. We see the other person in the golden glow of Aphrodite and are drawn to the love and beauty we feel. When recall of a past love does not focus on the negatives, when you can recall how it felt to express love and feel loved, yearnings to feel this again arise. When this is combined with an awareness that time is passing, it can generate a new receptivity to love and intimacy, at any age.

The Third Apple: Awareness of the Urge to Create

As the finish line approaches and Atalanta draws even with Hippomenes, he drops the third golden apple. For a split second, Atalanta hesitates. Should she cross the finish line and win the race, or pick up the apple and lose? She reaches for the apple just as Hippomenes crosses the finish line to win the race—and Atalanta.

When Aphrodite imbues the urge to have a baby with her alchemical attraction, the mother archetype (Demeter) teams up to divert a goal-focused woman who, up to now, was never fascinated by babies or desired one of her own. It is the longing plus the tug of instinct to be a mother that shifts a woman away from her career track, and lets others pass her by. Wanting to have a baby can become compelling and surprising to the woman who never knew before that it could be important to her. But when Aphrodite casts her spell in conjunction with (or in conspiracy with) Demeter, a baby becomes the longed-for beloved.

This is very different from thinking about having a baby to complete an image, or put a checkmark on a To Do list. Or, as is often the case, to live up to the expectations that you should want to have at least one baby and that, once you do, the children come first. For women who are archetypally maternal, being a mother or not being able to conceive a child are deep soul issues. When archetype and role come together, being maternal is soul-satisfying, a source of meaning. But when this is not who you are deep down, being a full-time mother leads to what Betty Friedan described in *The Feminine Mystique* (1963) as "the problem with no name." She describes women "who had it all"—a husband with a career, children, a house in the suburbs with all the modern conveniences—and had expectations that it would make them happy. When they were not happy, they blamed themselves. These were women who didn't find meaning living through their relationship roles—as Mrs. and Mother.

Now that women are expected to integrate work and personal life, often with the added necessity to work for financial reasons, women who want most of all to be mothers are deprived when they can't be full-time mothers and have to leave their children with others. On the other hand, non-maternal women who have a baby because it is expected of them and secondary to a career or to a cause, may hardly miss a step as they take a very short time out to have the baby, then put it in the arms of someone else and return to the race. Some women who know themselves and also know that children deserve more than they can give them make the decision to be childless by choice. They find, however, that they are put on the defensive by the expectations of others. Now there is an assertive counter-designation to "childless"—"child-free." Still, it takes self-knowledge and courage to make this choice, which may be honoring a deep commitment of these women to a calling or cause, or a deep knowledge that motherhood is not for them.

Aphrodite's third apple can be the one that draws an Atalanta woman toward her creative expression. She picks up the golden apple and quits the race, which, up to then, has been absorbing. She is drawn to do something that holds a promise of fulfilling a need in her that would not be fulfilled by a baby or by continuing on the same path. Once this particular golden apple affects her, the urge is to *create, not procreate*—to bring forth something out of her soul and her experience. It may be through a medium like painting, music, or writing that she becomes totally absorbed in for the pleasure and fascination of it. Or it may be a cause to which she now wants to commit her experience, talents, and passion, becoming as devoted to this and to making a difference through what she is doing as a maternal woman is toward her child.

Aphrodite's golden apples cast her spell on Atalanta from the beginning, when they are hidden in Hippomenes' waistband. Atalanta is receptive to Aphrodite's influence for many reasons. The immediate task no longer challenges her; it is just one more race that she can easily win. The race will also be the end of Hippomenes, however, who loves her, which may have touched her heart. When she sees him coming toward the starting line with his hands on his waistband, she is reminded of Meleager, which opens doors of memory that she had closed.

Memories from which you cut yourself off remain alive in your personal unconscious, temporarily forgotten but accessible. Glimmerings of them may appear in dreams, but until you are able to take your focus away from the activities in the outer world, there is little space in your psyche to remember. With memory come feelings, thoughts, and reflections. Interest in what may lie in the personal unconscious seems to open a gateway to the collective unconscious, to the language of symbols and the relevance of myths to personal life. I have been bringing you into this realm.

In the Roman version of Greek mythology, the underworld is presided over by Pluto, the lord of the underworld whose name refers to "riches underground." Whatever we have neglected to develop is there; our untended natural talent, sources of joy and pain through which we are connected to all humanity, the archetypal patterns common to us all. As the Roman poet Terence said: "Nothing human is foreign to me." When the third apple of Aphrodite symbolizes creativity, an Atalanta who chooses to pick it up will be drawn into the archetypal world, which deepens creativity, empathy, and understanding.

In *Goddesses in Everywoman* (1984), I place Aphrodite in a category all her own as the alchemical goddess. In her mythology, she has awesome and irresistible power. She can cause all mortals and divinities—except the virgin goddesses—to fall in love, to forget their usual concerns and bonds, and to conceive new life. She imbues an attraction with magnetic beauty and subjectivity, as in "beauty is in the eye of the beholder." She inspires poetry and persuasive speech, and symbolizes the transformative and creative power of love. She values emotional experiences with others more than either independence from others, which characterizes the virgin goddesses (Artemis, Athena, Hestia), or the qualities or bonds to others that define the vulnerable goddesses (Hera, Demeter, Persephone).

When Aphrodite's influence is felt, the present moment is all that matters. The focus is on the beloved person or object, or on creative work that is totally absorbing. Under Aphrodite's spell, time distortions occur. When you are with your beloved person or creative work, you lose track of time; hours can seem like minutes and a timeless moment can feel like the eternal now.

Women whose dominant archetypes are not the virgin goddesses are much more susceptible to Aphrodite. They are emotionally more vulnerable to falling in love without seeing the person clearly. They are more apt to become obsessed by another person, or to be dominated by a stronger personality, or to feel that their worth depends on having a defining relationship as spouse, lover, or mother. When Aphrodite is the dominant archetype in a woman, especially if she is attractive and young, she is often caught between the archetype in her (embodied, sensual, in the moment), and the consequences of being sexual and unwise (pregnancy, a bad reputation, victimized).

Until the footrace, Atalanta is not under the spell of an Aphrodite attraction. During the footrace, she undergoes an internal struggle between being in the race and winning it, or succumbing to the attraction of the apples and, with them, Hippomenes. She forgets that she is in the race and that the point is to win it. Each time Hippomenes throws a golden apple in her path, it distracts her focus. Then she remembers the race, sees that she is losing, and races to catch up. At the very end, however, Aphrodite prevails over the goal-oriented competitive focus of Artemis.

What do Aphrodite's apples mean to you? Awareness of time passing? Love and intimacy? A baby? Your own creativity? Or something else?

ATALANTA AND HIPPOMENES

When Atalanta reaches for Aphrodite's third golden apple, she loses the race. But she gets the apple and Hippomenes for her husband. Until this race, goal-focused, one-in-herself, competitive Atalanta identifies with Artemis. In real life, similar stories are brought to life through what appears to be an attraction of opposites. A man like Hippomenes, who falls in love with an Atalanta, may have admired her from a distance. He is probably not as ambitious or as accomplished as she is and doesn't compete with her or feel diminished by her. His love may include seeing and wanting to take care of her vulnerability, which she hides—from others and from herself. If that third apple arouses thoughts of having a child in an Atalanta, and if she is also affected by her ticking biological clock, she may notice Hippomenes' good-father qualities and be attracted to them. Time was when a warrior/defender or a bring-home-the-bacon provider fit the definition of a good match, but a successful Atalanta has these qualities herself.

People who still have a traditional, patriarchal notion of marriage expect a woman "to do better" than be with a man who makes less money than she does or has less education. They will be even more judgmental if he becomes the primary parent when they have children—if he is the one who goes to school conferences and stays home if a child is sick. While most Atalanta/Hippomenes unions are not complete role-reversal marriages, they usually are egalitarian and each fills some of the other's traditional roles.

An Atalanta is not attracted to patriarchal men who consider wives, and women in general, as possessions and adjuncts to their needs. When asked why she wasn't married, Gloria Steinem once said in an interview: "I don't mate well in captivity!" This was a question that assumed that any woman as attractive as she should have been chosen. Ordinary unmarried women are asked the same question, and often feel it tinged with the subtext: There must be something wrong with you. Men do the choosing, after all, and a woman's worth and role are based on this principle in most of the world and in many extended families.

Cultures with a male god at the top of the pantheon and men made in the image of that god do not consider women as equals, but as possessions. This is a viewpoint in transition in the United States, but it is one widely held and enforced in other more fundamentalist societies in the world. The difference archetypally between men, whom I categorize in *Gods in Everyman* (1989), is between those who identify primarily with the father archetypes (and tend to be patriarchal) and those who identify with the "generation of the sons" (more egalitarian). The patriarchal roles for women make her a daughter until she becomes a wife and then becomes a mother.

The patriarchal marriage is between two people who consider themselves almost different species, each conforming to the expectations or stereotypes of their gender. They divide responsibilities and psychological qualities between them. As husbands used to say: "She is my better half"—meaning that he goes into the competitive world and acts accordingly, while she stays at home and is the caretaker and nurturer, and is the more empathic and kinder half of the couple. Human qualities have a bell-curve distribution among male and female. Culture shapes which ones are acceptable in each gender and individuals learn which parts of themselves they should suppress to fit the acceptable stereotype. The qualities we develop result from nature *and* nurture, the matrix of genetic-archetypal and family-cultural influences.

The distribution of human qualities between men and women actually resembles two overlapping bell curves, in which some women (like Atalanta) have more of what men are supposed to have than a lot of men, and some men (like Hippomenes) have more qualities considered womanly than many women. Only when boys and girls, men and women, are free to develop whatever human qualities they have—the natural talents human children are endowed with that patriarchy assigns to one or the other of the genders (also failing to consider the in-between transgendered people among us)—are people free to be themselves. Researchers on empathy describe women as the empathic gender, but there are men who are more empathic than many women, just as there are women who are more goal-focused than many men.

The Inner Sacred Marriage—*Coniunctio*

Another way of looking at the marriage of Atalanta and Hippomenes is as an inner marriage, or *coniunctio* (which means "joining" in Latin), a concept developed by C. G. Jung. This refers to a union of opposites in the psyche that leads to wholeness. Jung's *anima/animus* concept postulated that every man has an *anima,* a feminine, in his psyche; likewise, every woman has a contra-sexual male aspect, or *animus.* These need to be brought into consciousness. In Jung's view, a man's anima and a woman's animus are, by definition, less conscious and therefore inferior to similar ego-developed qualities in the other gender. This theory works with men and women who have qualities that are typical of stereotyped roles. This is generally so if women are not educated and can't have responsibilities and authority in the world, and if men are not involved with young children, have no domestic responsibilities, and are discouraged from interests in the arts.

Typically male and typically female psychological patterns may apply to a majority or more of each gender, but do not fit a significant number on a normal bell curve of human qualities. Once these qualities are seen as part of a continuum, and not defined as either "masculine" or "feminine" in a binary system, then Atalanta and Hippomenes can be seen as an atypical, but normal, pair of opposites that attract each other. This attraction of opposites can be seen in same-sex couples as well.

Couples where both become unique and whole people often start out with each partner admiring something that is different from themselves as part of the attraction to the other. The potential of bringing something beautiful that exists in your unconscious into consciousness is an impetus toward wholeness, and part of the alchemical attraction that Aphrodite creates between two people whose differences attract the other person.

Not Happily Ever After

In versions of Atalanta's story that go back to ancient Greece, the myth doesn't end at the end of the race. Instead, almost as a postscript, we learn of the consequences that befall Hippomenes and Atalanta on their journey home.

Aphrodite is unhappy with Hippomenes, who has won Atalanta with her help. He forgets that he owes his wife (and his life) to Aphrodite and fails to honor her. At the very least, according to Ovid, he should give her thanks and burn incense in her temple. When he doesn't, the goddess feels slighted and becomes angry. To make matters much worse, when the couple stop for a rest at the temple of Cybele, Hippomenes is overcome with passion. Seeing a dimly lit cavern where priests placed their old wooden images, he makes love to Atalanta there. This is a desecration of an ancient temple, a sacrilege. For this, the lovers are changed into a pair of lions and forever yoked to Cybele's chariot. Aphrodite thus enjoys a delicious revenge, for it was believed at the time that lions did not mate with one another, but only with leopards—a very strange misconception. In any case, yoked as they are and pulling in traces together, the pair can not mate.

I think of this ending as a cautionary tale—one that metaphorically can lead to "persona marriages" when Aphrodite is not honored. These are marriages between two people who are lionized as a well-matched pair and who look the part in public. But between them in private, they are not emotionally intimate and love-making has become perfunctory and infrequent, or even non-existent. Aphrodite may have sparked the original attraction, but once settled into a routine or into the glamour or importance of their roles—or because of long hours, travel, the intensity of work, or children—intimacy fades. When the honeymoon is over and they are establishing themselves as homeowners, parents, and responsible members of the community, the couple can feel yoked together, harnessed to mortgages, student loans, and other financial burdens.

A woman physician spoke to me years ago after I had told this story, because in this she found a metaphor for her own marriage. She and her husband had a well-run household and a smoothly functioning partnership. I wonder: Did she speak to him about being lonely in the marriage, about the lack of emotional and physical intimacy, which she now wanted? Did he have any similar feelings? Was he dismissive or defensive? Could they speak together of vulnerabilities, disappointments, needs, and fears? What did each want of life and each other? Did they go into couple therapy? Was it possible to transform them from "lions" into intimates? Or did talking make it clear that they held irreconcilable expectations, as often happens between a patriarchal husband and his egalitarian wife. When this happens, even though the partners may be the same age, they may be a generation apart in attitude. Women who are archetypally Artemis may leave a conventionally good marriage for reasons that other women with different archetypes do not understand. This is perhaps what Jane Fonda, then around sixty, meant when she commented at one of the annual Omega conferences on her divorce from a man whose expectations of her limited who she could be: "I realized I could either die whole or die married."

ATALANTA IN *FREE TO BE YOU AND ME*

The name Atalanta is familiar to many women who, as children or as young mothers, remember Marlo Thomas' *Free to Be . . . You and Me*, which tells the story of the footrace ("Atalanta," by Betty Miles). The Princess Atalanta "was so bright, and so clever, and could build things and fix things so wonderfully, that many young men wished to marry her." There are too many men for the king to choose among, however. Atalanta says: "You don't have to choose, I will choose, and I'm not sure I'll marry anyone at all." The king discounts this last possibility, saying: "Of course you will . . . it's what people do."

With so many suitors to choose from, the king decides that he will hold a great race and give the winner the right to marry his daughter. Like the mythological Atalanta, she agrees to the race, but negotiates a condition: "Very well, but you must let me race along with the others." So the race with marriage as the prize is announced throughout the kingdom. Atalanta prepares for the race, getting up at dawn to practice running in secret, until she can run the course faster than anyone has ever run it before.

Meanwhile, one suitor—Young John, who has seen Atalanta at a distance—wants to earn the right to talk to her and become her friend. He thinks: "For sure, it is not right for Atalanta's father to give her away to the winner of the race. Atalanta herself must choose the person she wants to marry, or whether she wishes to marry at all." He also secretly practices running, until he can run the course faster than anyone has done before.

The day of the race, there are no golden apples. Many suitors race, but none can keep up with Atalanta except Young John. They reach the finish line and break through the golden ribbon together. The king then gives Young John the right to marry Atalanta, since he has come the closest to winning. Young John responds: "I could not possibly marry your daughter unless she wished to marry me. I have run this race for the chance to talk with Atalanta, and if she is willing, I am ready to claim my prize." The two talk, become friends, and go off separately to see the world.

This version of the Atalanta myth ends with: "Perhaps some day they will be married, and perhaps they will not. In any case, they are friends. And it is certain that they are both living happily ever after." I would add a postscript. It is likely that Atalanta and John are models for the generation of children who read this book and sang the songs—the Gen X and Millennials who had mothers influenced by the Women's Movement who raised them to be "free to be themselves."

"Living happily ever after" is a fairy-tale ending. What happens after "and they lived happily ever after" is what Stephen Sondheim's award-winning musical *Into the Woods* (1986) is about. All the fairy-tale characters must deal with what happens *after* "happily ever after." How does Jack, of beanstalk fame, deal with a dead giant in his back yard? Do Cinderella and Rapunzel marry princes and really end up having happy and fulfilling lives? Is carving up the wolf really the solution for Little Red Riding Hood? In real lives, there is unpredictability and routine. However, Atalanta and Young John have characters that will hold up in life. They have principles; they know what matters to them. And they are willing to work hard, and respect the sovereignty of each other. They will not take that which is not freely given, and they have a capacity for male/female friendship as equals.

Atalanta/Artemis women who know that their careers, creativity, or causes are their calling may heed Sheryl Sandberg's advice about relationships in *Lean In: Women, Work and the Will to Lead* (2013). While Sandberg writes about leadership in the outer world of institutions, I am writing about girls and women whose indomitable spirit leads them to have authentic and meaningful lives, however conventional or unconventional they may be—with or without a Meleager or Hippomenes. Sandberg writes:

> *I truly believe that the single most important career decision that a woman makes is whether she will have a life partner and who that partner is. I don't know of one woman in a leadership position whose life partner is not fully—and I mean fully—supportive of her career. No exceptions.*

Sandberg learned from her own experience and is now in the mutually supportive marriage she describes, after a brief previous marriage and divorce.

Chapter Seven

Virgin Goddess Archetype: Artemis, Athena, Hestia

Artemis, Athena, and Hestia are the three virgin goddesses of Greek mythology. The virgin-goddess archetype represents that part of a woman that is unowned by a man, untouched by a need for him or a need to be validated by him. It is that part of her that exists separate from a man, and from masculine collective opinion. The virgin is the inner woman who is one-in-herself, who can live in the privacy of a woman's inner life. Each of the three Greek virgin goddesses is different from the others in her qualities and values, but they all personify the independent and impersonal aspects of women's psychology. In this context, "virgin" means that there is a significant part of each that remains psychologically virginal, not that she is physically virginal.

The tie at the end of the footrace in the *Free to Be* version of Atalanta's story reflects what is happening between contemporary Atalanta women and Young John men now that both have equal opportunities to pursue personal interests, to excel, to compete with each other, and to be friends and postpone marriage. Cultural attitudes are in transition. In the myth, the king assumes rights over his daughter's life and her marriage. The king also claims the right to choose a husband for his daughter. In this king's world, everyone marries when they are supposed to, and daughters marry their fathers' choice. This is still true in parts of the world where marriages are formally arranged, often with a "bride price" or dowry. There are some underlying similarities when there are social and family expectations placed on a young woman to marry and to "marry well."

But "everybody" is not Atalanta. With Artemis as her major archetype, a woman may or may not marry or have children. When she does, a part of her remains one-in-herself, psychologically virgin. This is best described by Jungian analyst M. Esther Harding in *Woman's Mysteries* (1973):

> *A woman who is virgin, one-in-herself, does what she does—not because of any desire to please, not to be liked, or to be approved, even by herself; not because of any desire to gain power over an other, to catch his interest or love, but because what she does is true. Her actions may indeed be unconventional. She may have to say no, when it would be easier, as well as more adapted, conventionally speaking, to say yes. But as virgin she is not influenced by the considerations that make the non-virgin woman, whether married or not, trim her sails and adapt herself to expediency. I say married or not, for using the term virgin in its psychological connotation refers not to external circumstances but to an inner attitude.*

ARTEMIS

In previous chapters, Artemis has been described mostly through qualities in Atalanta. As Goddess of the Hunt and Moon, known to the Romans as Diana, she is portrayed as a tall lovely goddess, often in a short tunic holding a quiver of arrows and a bow, with a crescent moon and stars crowning her head. She prefers the wilderness and roams through virgin forests, meadows, mountains, and glades with nymph companions and hunting dogs.

Artemis is the archer with unerring aim, in pursuit of her own chosen quarry or target. A strong quality of women of this archetype is the ability to concentrate intensely on whatever is important to them, undistracted by the needs or judgment of others. Focus and perseverance are qualities of the archetype that make it possible to aim for and hit a self-chosen goal or mark. With her moonlight vision, Artemis, as Goddess of the Moon, can roam through woods, mountains, and meadows, touched by the mystery and beauty that moonlight brings to the landscape. Seeing the universe through the lens of this archetype, the universe and every element easily become part of a vast oneness; reverence and respect for all of nature and for indigenous spirituality comes naturally as well.

As the goddess of wildlife, Artemis has many undomesticated animals as symbols that reflect her qualities: the stag, doe, hare, and quail all share her elusive qualities; the lioness displays her regality and prowess as a hunter; the fierce boar shows her destructive aspect. The mother bear is the totem animal for her role as protector of the young. One derivation of the name Artemis is thought to be related to the bear. Where there were wild horses that roamed with companions, as Artemis did with her nymphs, the wild horse became another one of her symbols.

In her mythology, Artemis is the daughter of Leto and Zeus, a lineage of Titan nature divinities on her mother's side with her father the chief god of Mount Olympus. She is the first-born twin sister of Apollo, the God of the Sun. She is the only goddess who comes to the aid of her mother, which she does in several myths, even from the moment of her own birth. Artemis is appealed to for help by women in childbirth, for rescue from rapists, and as the protector of the young, especially of pre-adolescent girls. She is accompanied by a band of nymphs, minor feminine nature deities who are associated with woods, mountains, glades, lakes, and meadows. Artemis is the archetype of the sister, with brotherly feelings of equality with men and feelings of sisterhood with women. The mythology of Artemis the goddess and the concerns of women in whom "she" is the archetype reflect those of contemporary feminists.

Artemis Traits Show Up Early

The poet Callimachus describes how Artemis, at age three, is brought to meet her father, Zeus, for the first time. He is delighted with her, and says he will give her anything she wishes. Typical of Artemis, even at three, she knows exactly what she wants and tells him she wants to select them herself. She chooses a silver bow and arrows (as Katniss acquired for herself in *The Hunger Games*), hunting dogs, nature-nymph companions to roam with (a circle of friends—her sisterhood), the right to wear a short hunting tunic instead of a goddess gown (a preference for clothes that are functional and comfortable), eternal virginity (to stay one-in-herself), and the wilderness as her realm. Artemis charms her father with her spirit and certainty, much as daughters like her can and do please some fathers who are charmed by them.

This is a "Daddy's little girl," father/daughter vignette. Zeus is delighted with her, charmed by her, and supports her in being herself. He gives her permission and the means (bow and arrows) to achieve and to be independent; he allows her to choose her own friends and follow her own instinct or nose (hunting dogs) to go after what matters to her. He takes delight in her, which affirms her as a charming and attractive person and provides the basis for her having a positive sense of herself as a girl and later as a woman. She doesn't worry about being unfeminine, even as she does things that girls don't usually do. Early affirmation from a loving father provides this sense of self in his daughter.

Toddlers with an Artemis' power of concentration focus on what draws their interest. This often has to do with mastery of new challenges—from taking their first steps, to walking, jumping, and running, to finishing a puzzle or putting one block on top of another. They feel strongly about what is fair and what is not. They remember promises. As they grow older, they may come to the defense of someone smaller; they may speak up or stand up for the rights of someone else. They will have conflicts with men and women in authority and authoritarian institutions if they demand obedience based on having the power to enforce a "do what I say" attitude without a rationale. They may be punished as youngsters for asking questions, and may be told: "No back talk!" As a result, they may learn not to speak up or to show overt opposition. Nonetheless, they will continue to feel what they feel, and may keep the Artemis archetype alive in their imaginations through identifying with characters in stories. Intentions that begin with "when I grow up. . ." may keep them from feeling hopeless and helpless under the worst of circumstances.

Wonder Women

It used to be that the protagonists who resisted and prevailed were mostly male, so girls with the energy and focus of Artemis often imagined themselves as men. Wonder Woman emerged on the scene as a comic-book character in the Second World War. Through her, girls could imagine themselves as Diana Prince, who, in her secret identity as Wonder Woman—a princess of the Amazons with superpowers and skills who fought for justice, peace, love, and equality—could protect others and was invulnerable herself.

Shortly after World War II, Astrid Lindgren's Pippi Longstocking came on the scene. I came across an article by Connie Schulz in *Parade* magazine (February 24, 2013) with the title: "Three Cheers for Pippi!" The story began with Schulz claiming Pippi as "my favorite childhood hero—a scrappy little girl who asked a lot of questions and always put bullies in their place." Schulz wrote about yearning "for a fiery spirit which would embolden mine." She found red-haired Pippi Longstocking. "What I most loved was her intolerance for bullies," she explains. "She hurled them into trees and onto rooftops—with one arm. I still harbor that fantasy."

For six years in the mid-1990s, Xena the Warrior Princess fought on the side of good on television. By the beginning of the 21st century, there were many portrayals of young women and girls who had Artemis/Atalanta qualities. Besides Katniss in *The Hunger Games*, there is Princess Merida in *Brave*, an animated feature-length movie about a free-spirited sixteen-year-old who is expected to marry one of the three young first-born sons of Clan lords who have come to compete in an archery contest for her hand. She upsets the situation by declaring herself eligible as a first-born, and defeats them all. The bear symbol is prominent throughout this story. Merida's mother and triplet young brothers are transformed into bears and back into human form in the knick of time. The Lords of the Clans agree that, from now on, there will be no more arranged marriages or marriages by contest, and that their children will be free to get married in their own time to whomever they please.

Artemis and Retribution

There is one myth of Artemis in which her privacy is violated. The hunter Actaeon is hunting in the forest with his dogs when he comes upon Artemis bathing in a pond with her nymph companions. He stares at her nakedness, gawking like a Peeping Tom at this most private of goddesses whom no man or god could ever possess. Artemis immediately throws water in his face, transforming him into a stag. No longer recognizing him, his dogs attack. Actaeon flees for his life, but is taken down by the hounds and torn to pieces.

Women with the Artemis archetype are quick to action and quick to punish a specific person for a specific offense.

This side of Artemis differs from the indiscriminate rage expressed through the Calydon boar. Artemis also uses her bow and arrows on specific targets—for instance, to punish the arrogant woman who demeans her mother's honor and to save her mother from being raped.

Lisbeth Salander, protagonist in Stieg Larsson's Millennium series, is a fictional example of a "raped non-victim." She comes under the control of a court-appointed guardian who sexually abuses her and has absolute power over her freedom. Salander bides her time, until she can brilliantly punish her rapist. She has the focused arrows and passion for retributive justice of Artemis and the strategy of Athena.

Artemis As Activist

With the spirit and energy of the Artemis archetype, women become activists for feminism and social justice—against bullies of all kinds, perpetrators of rape, domestic violence, oppression of the poor and powerless—as well as environmentalists, defenders of wildlife, and tree huggers. Women with an archetypal kinship with Artemis are called into action by outer events and an inner response to do something about them. This is what makes women—those who have suffered as well those who have not—come to the aid of others. Mother-bear outrage is evoked by abuse of power; mother-bear protection rises to defend those who are being abused, trashed, or violated, especially the young and vulnerable. One of the characteristics of the Artemis archetype is to take action, just as the goddess does in her mythology. She is the archetype in the feminist activist, or animal activist, or nature activist, or social-justice activist whose instinct is to intervene.

Lisa Shannon, the once-casual runner who began Run for the Congo, tells of an incident that exemplifies this:

> *. . . there was that time after a gym-class volleyball game, during my freshman year of high school, when I noticed a group of boys swarming around the net. It was another problem with Trevor Samson, the school geek. This time he was in a verbal sparring match with a popular kid . . . We weren't friends. I didn't like him. He was a nerd's nerd: obnoxious. Vulnerable. Pathetic. The confrontation heated up. More than thirty boys, mostly of the West Hills breed, had gathered around and were egging on the aggressor. They wanted to see a fight. Without considering the social risk, I pushed my way past the pack and stepped between Trevor and Mr. Popular. I stuck my finger in Chip or Chard or Seth's face and declared, "Stop!" A kid with chiseled features and glowing tan shouted from the herd, "Shut up you f---ing hippie bitch!" I stood my ground, squarely in front of Trevor, shielding him with the hard fact there is no social status to be gained from hitting a girl. The crowd disbanded.*

Lisa's story reminded me of a time in which I felt I had to speak up. I was twelve and belonged to the Youth Group at my church. The adult leader of the group made a slanderous comment about Jews, which was offensive—especially from him as a Christian leader. I don't remember specifics, but I do recall that hypocrisy was the issue and that I spoke up and confronted him. Then I quit the group and went to another church. A similar provocation and response resulted in my spending an uncomfortable time in the vice-principal's office in high school. I refused to back down and take back what I had said about favoritism and discrimination to the sponsor of the tenth-grade school organization that was supposed to be open to all. I agreed to apologize for *how* I had said what I said, but would not take back *what* I had said. This, while not what the vice-principal wanted to hear, was enough for her to let me go. I learned three years later that this resulted in my not getting into Stanford, when my father went to bat for me and went to the Dean of Admissions to learn why I was turned down. The reason turned out to be the "dinging" letter sent by that vice-principal.

That my father would make an appointment and fly up to Stanford hoping to reverse their decision moves me still. He "had my back." From this experience and others, I learned how our paths through life are labyrinthine. Walking the Chartres labyrinth is instructive. While there are no dead ends, there are twenty-eight 180-degree U-turns, which are part of the journey. I spent a semester at UCLA, then transferred mid-semester to Pomona College, where I spent two very good years in one of the best small liberal arts colleges in the country. Then, after a summer fulfilling a pre-med physics requirement at UC Berkeley and on finding that I loved being there, I transferred mid-semester in my Junior year. I graduated from UC Berkeley and went on to UC San Francisco Medical School.

Recently, I went to my class reunions at Pomona College and at UC Berkeley, which reminded me of how rich the experiences and friendships at both places had been. Who knows where the path denied to me by that vice-principal would have led me? But I do know that these shifts in direction required making choices that exercised the qualities of self-determination that are part of my Artemis archetype and a childhood pattern in which I coped well.

It was probably my checkered school career in childhood that made moving from one college to another not very difficult. Between kindergarten and the fourth grade, I was enrolled in seven different schools, including schools in Los Angeles, Kew Gardens New York, Black Foot Idaho where children from the reservation were bused in, Grand Junction and Denver Colorado, and Monrovia California. Then it was back to Los Angeles, where we settled down and I could progress with classmates through the remainder of elementary school, junior high school, and high school. Many children of those in the military, or in the corporate world, or in diplomatic postings have had to adjust to many moves and many schools. Now that I'm familiar with UN designations, I think we could qualify as "internally displaced refugees."

My family left the Los Angles area to escape the evacuation and relocation of all people of Japanese ancestry to internment camps, where we would have been kept behind barbed wire in tar-papered barracks in desolate places in the Western states. It did not matter that we were American citizens. My parents were born and educated in the United States; my father was a businessman, my mother a physician. Our first move was to Del Rey, California, just before those of Japanese ancestry were placed under martial law in Los Angeles.

Once out of California, we were again free American citizens. Our subsequent many moves were necessitated by other circumstance and my father's efforts to get his parents and siblings out of the camps. Meanwhile, I was enrolled in one school after another—often the only child with a Japanese face—while our country was at war with Japan. Families' lives are also disrupted in economic recessions, as parents seek jobs elsewhere. Children cope with the moves, with new schools, and with temporary housing. These experiences support the development of Artemis and Athena archetypes in girls—just as being an internally displaced refugee did for me. It also gave me a first-hand experience of and an interest in social justice and racism.

Virgin Goddesses and Non-Victims

In their mythologies, the three virgin goddesses are not overpowered, raped, or humiliated. While these goddesses are immune to abuse, women in whom these virgin goddesses are active archetypes can be abused and raped. According to Amnesty International, one in every three women in the world will be raped or brutally beaten in their lifetime. The indomitable spirit of Artemis in women need not be subdued by rape, however. Instead of becoming shamed victims, women with the Artemis archetype seek justice or vengeance, become even more determined to pursue their calling, and are not stopped by the rape. Artemis is the archetype that helps women to survive violence against them. Artemis is that part in the psyche of women that can remain unpenetrated and unsubdued—even when abused, raped, or trafficked. These are women who then volunteer to rescue others and help them to heal. While their bodies are violated, their souls are not.

Lara Logan, CBS News Foreign Correspondent on *60 Minutes,* was described as a "rape non-victim" after the horrifying gang rape she suffered in the middle of Cairo's Tahrir Square during the Arab Spring revolts in 2011. That she was able to muster the character, strength, and survival skills to get through this physical and psychological ordeal surprised Logan. "You don't realize until it happens to you that you have a choice not to fall apart," she said. "I have too much to live for." Logan was rescued by women in the square and by twenty uniformed soldiers. While in the midst of it, she not only thought she was going to die, but that it would also be a tortuous death. She felt as if her limbs were being torn off as 200 to 300 men grabbed at her and raped her with their hands. Rather than have CBS issue an ambiguous statement that she had been attacked, Logan insisted that the statement detail how she was beaten and sexually assaulted.

Logan is described by her boss as obsessive in her determination to go to any length to get a story. Before the invasion of Iraq, she refused to evacuate with her CBS team and only briefly decamped to the border of Jordan at her boss's insistence. She then drove back into "shock and awe," blaring Van Morrison all the way. Logan has established deep contacts with the military and her stories are "based on trust and knowledge." Says Logan: "Most of the time the military absolutely hates the media; breaking through that barrier is very hard." She poured herself into covering two wars, and has not stopped covering the Middle East. After she recovered from the sexual assault, she returned to cover news in Afghanistan.

It's clear from Lara Logan's reputation and achievements that she has Artemis traits. The targets she aims for are the stories she writes. To get them, she travels into war zones and has gained the respect of military men who mistrust most journalists and won't talk to them. Lara and all others who have been raped but not subdued as victims retain the one-in-herself core of the archetype. Her body could be violated. She thought she was about to die, but something in her remained virgin, one-in-herself, untamed by the abuse, thanks to the indomitable spirit of Artemis and her affinity with the warrior aspects of Athena, who could keep her head and be objective in the midst of a battlefield.

Margaret Talbot's article "Gone Girl," published in *The New Yorker* (October 21, 2013), focused on the extraordinary resilience of Elizabeth Smart, who was abducted from a bedroom in her family's home in Salt Lake City when she was fourteen and kept for nine months in captivity. During that time, she was repeatedly raped and threatened with murder; finally, she was rescued by the police. Her memoir, *My Story* (2013)—along with those of Jaycee Duggard (abducted at age eleven), Natascha Kempusch in Austria, and Sabine Dardenne in Belgium—is an appalling account of abuse and survival. All these women did what they had to do to survive. In summing up, Talbot wrote that they displayed "an elemental will to live that is deeply affecting."

In Elizabeth Smart's case, it required a tremendous physical stamina to live through her captivity. "She had been an athlete as a kid: she had been a runner, and had ridden horses in the Wasatch Mountains." Elizabeth recalled: "I was no body-builder, but I was no weakling, either." Eleven years after her abduction, Elizabeth is married and has become a full-time advocate for the prevention of child abuse. She lobbies for legislation, heads a foundation, and gives about eighty speeches a year. Speaking to teenagers at the Key Club International conference, she ended her talk with this: "Never be afraid to speak out. Never be afraid to live your life. Never let your past dictate your future."

Just as these women triumphed over rape, Carole Comeau triumphed over circumstances. When Comeau read Lara Logan's statement about choosing not to fall apart, the words took her back to a moment of truth in which she was almost overcome but didn't fall apart. Carole was flying solo in Alaska, a step toward meeting the requirements to get a pilot's license. Her task was to fly over 200 miles, landing and taking off from three different airports. The runways were icy; the weather was turning bad and getting worse. As the wind buffeted the small plane, she was "blubbering and telling herself, 'I can't do this.'" She remembers the moment when she made a choice not to fall apart. As she held back tears so she could see the gauges, she stopped saying "I can't" and instead told herself to "suck it up!" As she flew that little plane, her message to self was: "There's no one else here; it's up to you!" She took charge, not knowing whether she would make it to a safe landing or not. "I had no other option if I didn't want to die." She and others who find the core one-in-herself strength not to be overcome in circumstances where giving up would be fatal, literally know the meaning of the saying: "That which does not kill us makes us strong." (Friedrich Nietzsche)

The decision not to fall apart is one that women and girls make under much less dramatic situations all the time. Many girls with Atalanta qualities have an inbred determination not to cry when the bigger people around them are insensitive or mean. The archetype in them refuses to act the part of a victim. They may be beaten, but their indomitable spirits are unbowed.

GODDESS-ARCHETYPE PATTERNS

Artemis, Athena, and Hestia can be appreciated as distinct archetypal patterns in themselves. Their aspects can co-exist within the same woman along with other archetypes, representing the three stages of a woman's life. Artemis is the most youthful. Practical and competent Athena, the goddess who never lost her head or her heart, is the personification of a sensible adult. Quiet and centered Hestia easily steps into the role of wise woman and crone in later years. These archetypes can exist simultaneously in any woman throughout her life, or can emerge as important at a particular stage in life.

The virgin goddesses are impervious to Aphrodite and Eros. This is what makes them unique. No others—whether an Olympian deity or a mortal—could resist Eros' arrows. However, the mortal women in whom these archetypes are active are not impervious. When they fall in love, the archetypes of Artemis, Athena, or Hestia remain unaffected. These women, however, are not the archetype and can love deeply. They do not fall in love as easily or unconsciously as women whose predominant archetypes are Aphrodite or the three goddesses I categorize as the vulnerable goddesses—Hera (Goddess of marriage, archetype of wife), Demeter (Goddess of grain, archetype of the mother), and Persephone (mother's daughter) who was abducted into the underworld. With strong one-in-herself archetypes, these women are less likely to project an expectation of being fulfilled, rescued, taken care of, or made complete by having a spouse, child, or lover. The other archetypes may become active, as often happens when a desire to have a baby arises in a woman who was previously focused on career or education or adventures (one meaning of the third golden apple that Atalanta picked up, letting Hippomenes win the race). When striving to win or to excel loses its importance, shifts in the inner world and choices in the outer world change.

The desire to settle down—to have a home or husband/intimate or baby—is a desire that may fluctuate, being strongest during the progesterone phases (second half) of a woman's menstrual cycle. With strong virgin-goddess archetypes, a woman is unlikely to be taken over by her longing for what she does not have. She may be married, or marry more than once. She may never marry; she may remain a virgin; she may have many lovers. She may have children and love them very much; but, since she does not need to be a mother to give her life meaning, she helps them to grow up rather than keeping them dependent on her.

An archetype is a pattern and each Greek goddess archetype has recognizable characteristics that fit that pattern. However, a woman is much more than her major archetype or archetypes. She is unique, like her fingerprint. She may have similarities in common with others who may begin with the same configuration of archetypes, but the family, culture, and time in which she lives will have a lot to do with what her options are.

Women in whom the vulnerable goddesses and Aphrodite (whom I place in her own category as the alchemical goddess) are strong find that their relationships are sources of both meaning and suffering. In their mythologies, the vulnerable goddesses are overpowered, abducted, raped, depressed, and obsessed, susceptibilities shared by women in whom they are the strongest archetypes. In contrast, Artemis and Athena are more likely to cause others who care about them to feel rejected or unimportant, especially if, like Atalanta, they were unmothered and had to raise themselves much of the time. Consistency of love is not something these women know much about, so they can't provide it to others until they learn empathy and compassion. Often, they need to become vulnerable themselves, either because they have become totally dependent for a time on another—after an accident, for example, or by letting their defenses down gradually as they learn to trust someone who loves them. Until then, they can be like mermaids—Esther Harding's descriptive image for attractive women who seem to attract people to them by instinct and yet are emotionally unfeeling when they respond (*Woman's Mysteries*, 1973). Mermaids are creatures who are half woman—warm and attractive—and half fish—impersonal or cold-blooded.

The intensity of involvement in something subjectively important to her can make an Artemis unavailable to those closest to her who expected more constancy. Like wildlife in the forest, there can be a "now you see her, now you don't" elusiveness about her. So real and present one moment, gone the next and not heard from for long stretches of time. Athena's lack of presence is of a different sort, which can be equally difficult for those who love her or want more of her. She leaves them by going into her head. When her mind is working on something, she may spend hours at her desk and computer, in her laboratory, or out in the field where her project is. She can be located physically, which may be a constant, but this is not enough when you want her attention.

By contrast, Hestia's one-in-herself quality is introverted. She is content to be in the peaceful, often sacred, spaces she creates. And though she is easy to be with and there is often a warmth about her, she seems difficult to know because she doesn't share much about herself—not because she is withholding, but because this is who she is. Each of these virgin-goddess qualities are part of an archetypal pattern, and women who personify these traits are being true to their archetypes. The result is that what they do is meaningful to them, but harder for others who want more of them or more intimacy with them.

Hestia

Hestia, Goddess of the Hearth and Temple, is the least known and the third virgin goddess in the Olympian pantheon. She is the first-born of Rhea and Cronos, and so is the eldest sister to the first generation of Olympians and maiden aunt to the second. Zeus is her brother, which makes Artemis and Athena her nieces. She is not portrayed in paintings or sculptures, and there are no myths about her, other than the one in which she asks for and receives eternal virginity and is given honors as well.

Neither images nor stories define Hestia. Instead, she is present as the sacred fire in the center of a round hearth. It is her presence that creates the sacred space in the house and temple. Her fire provides heat and light, and also is the fire over which food is cooked. These are metaphors for emotional warmth, spiritual illumination, and nourishment. A sacred fire in the center of a round hearth is also a geometric image of a mandala, Jung's image of the Self, and Tibetan Buddhism's sacred mandala paintings.

Women who personify Hestia qualities are one-in-themselves and introverted. They are in the present, neither holding on to the past nor anticipating the future. They are most comfortable with anonymity. It is the psychological place and inner attitude that people seek in meditation. I call Hestia the archetype of meditative wisdom in *Goddesses in Older Women* (2001). As children, Hestia women are often the least noticed in a large family or classroom. When Hestia is the dominant archetype, women usually avoid dramas in interpersonal relationships. Because they are naturally introverted, they can be detached; they may not have to strive and struggle with issues that others may have. This archetype provides spiritual, meditative, mystical, and psychological centering. Hestia's presence is invoked to make a women's circle a sacred space, when a candle is lit in the center and the members of the circle spend time together in prayer or meditation.

Since the Women's Movement, women who are archetypally Artemis and/or Athena (and the rest of them as well) can thrive in an extroverted world and may only glimpse yearnings from Hestia for introverted time. Hestia is the goddess who can become most important in the psyche in the third phase of life. This happens most commonly when an Artemis or Athena passses through menopause, wants to be one-by-herself, or enters a phase of her life when she lives alone. When Hestia stirs in you, solitude calls to you and nourishes your soul. To have the house to yourself or to get away by yourself feels wonderfully spacious.

A Guided Imagery for Hestia

Invite Hestia into your meditation as a visual and felt image. Imagine that there is a sacred fire glowing and warm in the center of your chest (the area of the heart chakra, under the end of your sternum, between your breasts). Take some slow deep breaths and let yourself relax and be at peace. If you want to, you can further imagine soft firelight and warmth spreading through your body; imagine lighting up the other chakras, which then also glow.

Here's an even simpler exercise. Once you are in a meditative, receptive, spacious state of mind, imagine yourself walking across a threshold and going through a doorway into Hestia's round temple. Sit, look into her fire, and be receptive to the thoughts, feelings, or images that come to you.

Going Solo

In women whose other archetypes are active and fulfilled through the mid-adult years, sovereignty may not become important until the second half or last third of life. Women happily devote themselves to children or marriage when this is so and circumstances make it possible. Their sovereignty may also be limited by economics and loyalty. The virgin-goddess archetypes may, in effect, need to wait their turn. In *Going Solo: The Extraordinary Rise and Surprising Appeal of Living Alone* (2012), Eric Klinenberg, professor of sociology at New York University, describes how living alone allows people to pursue sacred modern values—including individual freedom, personal control, self-realization, and time and space for restorative solitude. In other words, those so inclined archetypally and able to exercise personal choice are now "free to be." His point is that living alone, being alone, and feeling lonely are not the same experiences.

The *Time* article that introduced me to Klinenberg's work is "Living Alone is the New Norm" (March 12, 2012). It was based on the 2011 census: people who live alone—nearly 15 million Americans—make up 28% of all households. Solos are now tied with childless couples as the most prominent residential type, more common than the nuclear family, the multigenerational family and the roommate or group home. Moreover, those living alone were more likely to remain in their current state than anyone else except couples with children. Nearly everyone who lives alone has other less-expensive options, but opts to go solo.

The statistics surprised me, although I was not surprised at Klinenberg's conclusions, since I have observed and heard and know myself that many women in the second half and last third of life find living alone soul-satisfying. Living alone often allows women a luxury they never had before—of deciding how to spend their time. They can pursue their own interests—to make a difference, to support a cause, to be creative, to enjoy intellectual or spiritual pursuits, to keep their own hours, to spend quality time with their friends, grown children, or grandchildren, to make travel decisions, or just to stay in touch with people who matter to them but are not close by through all the communication technology now available. Or it may be that they are actively involved in their work in the world, and are glad to come home to the restorative solitude of being alone.

For many in the last half or last third of their lives, it may be the first time that they have a place of their own. They may have lived with parents, or roommates, or husbands and, only after divorce or widowhood do they find themselves unexpectedly by themselves in good archetypal company. An Artemis/Atalanta discovers Hestia in herself or has time for the intellectual pursuits of Athena. This is especially so in the third phase of life, when community colleges and universities are offering stimulating non-credit courses to older students who attend them simply for the love of learning.

Living alone is often initiated by divorce at midlife. In the usual variation of woman-as-victim, the woman may have been "dumped" by a husband who replaces her with a younger woman. In reality, most (statistics vary from two thirds to 90 percent) divorces and separations are initiated by women. When being a wife is a strong archetype (Hera, Goddess of Marriage and archetype of the wife), women who are widowed or divorced may too soon dwell upon finding a new partner and neglect themselves, ignoring the lessons learned from past relationships. It takes time to heal and grieve, to learn to be on your own, to develop a network of friends when being a couple and doing everything as a couple is a social requirement. But it can be delightful to find that solitude nourishes you through whatever it is that absorbs you—so much so that you lose track of time and look forward to having time alone. This does not mean that you will remain single, but rather that you will be fine if the right person does not come into your life.

PARADOX AND SYNCHRONICITY

Paradoxically, if the virgin-goddess archetypes are active and living alone is fine for you, a marriage or committed relationship that suits both partners may come about more easily. Consciously cultivating Hestia can lead to some discoveries—finding that you can be good company for yourself, developing or deepening interests of your own, or cultivating an inner life or a meditative practice, which may turn out to be an unintentional good strategy for finding love. When the lack of a relationship doesn't define you to yourself, that's when someone who may be a partner may arrive. The paradox is that, when you are no longer needy for someone to fill an empty space in your life, the possibility for someone coming into your life who enhances it increases—if it is to be at all. Over the decades I have had a psychotherapy/analytic practice, I've become more impressed by this observation: When the woman is ready, the partner will come (an adaptation of the Eastern saying: When the pupil is ready, the teacher will come). This has proven true more often than any statistical or experiential data about the lack of good men or women who are available.

It was easy for me to find an example in my own women's circle. I thought of Carole Robinson, who left Philadelphia for California and began anew following the end of a twenty-year relationship and the transition that followed. The impetus to venture into new terrain when her life in the old one ceased to have meaning had not led Carole to a major geographical move before this. But the pattern of taking a next step and doing what had meaning for her became strong in her new situation. A year after she arrived, Carole became the program director of Bread and Roses, a non profit begun by Mimi Farina to bring musicians to people who can not leave the institutions in which they live to go to performances. The group has been responsible for bringing musicians to prisons, nursing homes, and rehabilitation centers. This avocation was a good fit for Carole, and she stayed with it until her life took another turn—she got married.

Carole felt drawn to California, among other reasons, as a place where she could have a more spiritual life—Marin County offers many possibilities in this direction. She had lived alone for twelve years when she met Zane Gresham. There was a "vital charge," an attraction, between them and an intention that the relationship would begin as a friendship in which they would be authentic. They agreed that they would say what was true and be true to themselves in relationship with each other. Seven years ago, when Carole was sixty-two, the members of our women's circle were attendants at their marriage at Grace Cathedral. (The range of our ages made the term "bridesmaids" an inappropriate description and . . . "bridecrones?!" Zane referred to us as "the goddesses.") Symbols of the sacred feminine were interwoven into what we wore and carried, and in how the church was decorated for the ceremony.

When I told Carole that I was writing about Atalanta and thought her story made a point, she told me that she and her kids, Sara and Rob, could sing all the songs in *Free to Be You . . . and Me*. Sara recently found the album at a flea market and had it copied onto a disk so Carole could sing along with her grand-daughter. In the words from the song, Carole has become "the woman she was meant to be."

Shadow Aspects of the Virgin Archetypes

The virgin-goddess archetypes have negative potentials, or "shadow" aspects, that have an effect on others. Those who find themselves on the receiving end of Artemis' anger, whether sharply focused as retribution or out-of-control rage, know this shadow aspect, which can be without mercy. To grow beyond this, they must experience vulnerability and learn to forgive. When Athena sits in a seat of power, she can "turn people to stone." Her demands for logical explanations or justification may be her way to learn or assess a situation. She may be unaware that the combination of the power she has and the way she asks questions can make others inarticulate and unable to explain themselves. In her mythology, Athena wore the head of the gorgon Medusa on her breastplate, which had the power of turning anyone who gazed at it to stone. Until an Athena feels vulnerable herself, or has had an inexplicable, awe-evoking, numinous experience, she has no tolerance for anyone's experience of the invisible or mysterious. Emotional motivation may escape her understanding.

The goddess Athena was the best ally to have on the battlefield, because she never lost her cool and always thought strategically. The shadow aspect enters when her "do whatever works to win" attitude doesn't consider collateral damage or the morality of taking unfair advantage. This archetype in women can act as these goddesses did, without compassion or empathy. From childhood on, learning comes through the reactions of others. They serve as mirrors in which we can see how others see us. Growth in compassion and consciousness results from seeing our shadows and changing. The negative effect on others, and pain from rejection by others for our behavior, motivates change, as does a growth in imagination. When you can imagine how it would feel to be the other person, you have grown beyond these two archetypes.

Focused concentration is a quality of consciousness that, like a beam of light, illuminates only what it shines on. It, in effect, takes no notice of anything outside this focus. To feel what others may be feeling, to be able to understand why people do what they do, takes compassion and empathy. Women are called the empathic gender because we, in general, have this quality—as compared to men, who generally do not. Compassion and empathy do not, however, come as naturally to an Artemis or Athena—and possibly not to a Hestia, who must learn vulnerability and the necessity of taking other people's feelings into consideration, something that good parenting and deeper adult relationships teach.

Qualities of the one-in-herself archetypes can be obstacles to intimacy and vulnerability. To be absorbed in your world and not expect affirmation or love from others because, like Atalanta, you did not get it from parents supports the independence and autonomy that the virgin-goddess archetypes foster. These qualities do not round you out as a whole person who can love and be loved, trust and be vulnerable. Lessons in vulnerability and trust then often come through the pain you inadvertently cause others who love you and feel what you felt as a child—as if they don't matter. Good human parents are not perfect parents, but they provide you with a foundation of knowing that you and your feelings matter. People who love you provide this too. Remember the thoughts of Atalanta as she picked up the second apple in the footrace? Would it have been better not to have loved Meleager at all? Is intimacy worth the risk? Would it be better not to love at all?

Growing Beyond Archetype

There are growing pains involved in "growing human" through love and vulnerability. To grow beyond dominant virgin-goddess archetypes, especially if Artemis or Athena got you through a difficult childhood and adolescence, takes courage of a different kind than standing up against power or accepting intellectual challenges. Once you care deeply about someone, it is a risk. It may bring back painful experiences of loss, like Atalanta remembering Meleager's death. And yet, it is important that you remember those times when you were loved and someone noticed and cared if you were sad or hurt. Can you remember when you felt the security of love from a parent, grandmother, older sibling, good friend, or first love? This may have happened before you armored yourself against caring about people who could leave or betray you, before you gave up on needing humans and turned to nature and animals or to books and intellectual certainties. It may have been your animals who comforted you and whose care you provided and learned from. Courage comes from the French word *coeur*, meaning "heart." Once a woman who has prided herself on her physical or moral courage realizes that love relationships are risks of a different kind—harder for her to accept than for women she may not have admired before—new respect grows in her and new humility. This is part of her lessons.

The goddess Artemis responded to vulnerability—young animals, young humans, vulnerable mothers. And true to this archetype, it is through love for those who are vulnerable and initially dependent on them that women grow beyond the archetype through their own vulnerability. Motherhood stretches the heart, patience, and psyche of a one-in-herself archetypal woman—especially an Artemis who was "unmothered" herself. Sometimes this growth of love and how to mother comes from the practice she has as a devoted caretaker of her animals. It is through mothering their own babies that many women also mother the baby in themselves.

A woman who missed this experience of being mothered when she was a little girl can give this attentive love to her child when she becomes a mother, especially if she nurses her baby—instinctively entering the Madonna-and-child archetypal bubble of oneness with her child. When a woman with Artemis or Athena archetypes makes the choice to be a mother, to cherish this particular child or each one, motherhood can, over time, become a spiritual practice of humility and sacrifice (of what she otherwise would be doing)—through daily practice of unconditional love without immediate gratification, through daily maintenance, and through patience. This is especially so for one-in-herself women, for whom having a child is not a deep need, but rather a commitment. They develop constancy in the relationship in response to their children's needs and the love that this bond evokes in them. It is a commitment that will take much longer than a decision to walk the length of the Pacific Crest Trail, or bike alone from Seattle to San Diego. And while generally not recognized as such, when consciously made, this is a heroic commitment, especially when it gets hard and you are on your own. It's equivalent and more to telling yourself: "You decided to do this; get back on the bike and keep pedaling!"

Athena and Artemis as Allies

Looking back from a perspective of seventy years, I am aware that I grew up and entered my early adult years at the same time that the Women's Movement of the late 1960s and 1970s was changing the psychological landscape for women, raising consciousness, and changing our world. During the first years of the movement, I was in medical school, out of touch with much of what was going on in the outside world. This was followed by a demanding internship and a residency in psychiatry. I married James Bolen in the last year of my residency, started a private practice, and began as a candidate to become an analyst at the C. G. Jung Institute in San Francisco. In 1970, which began the decade of the Women's Movement, I had my first of two children—fittingly, a daughter, because it was this pregnancy, labor, and delivery that initiated me into a deep appreciation of my identity as a woman. Like all women, not an exception, just more privileged.

While I was active in college and medical school in extra-curricular activities, the social-justice/feminist activist did not stir in me until, as a psychiatrist, I led a protest against the American Psychiatric Association's failure to support the Equal Rights Amendment. The fact that inequality, discrimination, inferior status, and lack of opportunities all contribute to low self-esteem made this a mental health issue that I felt strongly about. I was warned that this was a bad career move at the time. It actually wasn't, as it turned out. It also led to meeting Gloria Steinem and to a realization that women psychiatrists both in favor of and against this issue differed in their dominant archetypes. This was a major insight that contributed to my writing *Goddesses in Everywoman*.

All of us underwent a similar vigorous training to become doctors, followed by years more of psychiatric training. We were now active in our professional organization, which at the time was 89 percent men. Those who felt a bond of sisterhood worked on women's issues and on behalf of women patients. These are qualities I associate with the Artemis archetype. They are not Athena loyalties or priorities. In her mythology, Athena emerges as a grown woman in golden armor from the head of Zeus, and is the only Olympian he trusts with his symbols of power. She is the Goddess of Wisdom (as strategy) and Crafts (practical arts like weaving). She is rational, unemotional, armored by intellect, trusted by Zeus, and mentor to heroes who go after what they want. Athena trusts patriarchal institutions and looks up to those at the top—who, then as now, are usually men.

When I wrote *Goddesses in Everywoman* (1984), the archetypal difference between Artemis and Athena was active in women on each side of a feminist divide. Athena archetypes supported patriarchal values; Artemis archetypes opened doors of opportunity that had been closed to women. Then Athenas, who seemed to have no sense of sisterhood, walked through those doors. In the intervening years, many women in the mold of Athena ran into glass ceilings, found discrimination in pay and advancement, discovered misogyny, and got a first-hand experience of what feminists had been saying. With reflection, Athena women may even have discovered that they were prejudiced against women themselves. As with internalized racism or homophobia, being in a patriarchal culture and accepting its values means thinking of women as inferiors and of yourself as an exception—until discrimination affects you. Now, both archetypes often seem internally related in women who lead with either Artemis or Athena.

My actions, decisions, and reactions are very Artemis. What I feel intuitively—the rightness and wrongness of something, fairness, looking out for the underdog—are deep principles. My current activism is as a persevering advocate for a fifth UN World Conference on Women (5WCW). I think of this as "my assigment"; it is a cause that is personally meaningful to me, one that engages my heart and mind, one done with others who share the same vision and goal. I see the conference as a step toward the tipping point at which the empowerment and equality of women will bring about a mothers' agenda. Once all mothers have what we want for our own children, real change can come about in the world. Athena is a strong presence in my psyche as an inner counselor. Athena is sensible. She bases decisions on thinking clearly about timing, energy, and available support.

Sheryl Sandberg's *Lean In: Women, Work, and The Will to Lead* (2013) is a prime example of this alliance between Artemis and Athena. She's the Chief Operating Officer at Facebook, working with founder Mark Zuckerberg and others in an environment that seems more circular than hierarchical—more brother/sister than the usual corporate model of "founding father," which hardly fits either the man or the style in which the company seems to function. Sandberg drew fire from some feminists for her advice about negotiating work and personal lives, and from some women's-circle activists for creating Lean In circles. She says: "[as a child,] as sappy as it sounds, I hoped to change the world." With facts and logic and personal anecdotes, she passes on what she has learned—one sister to another. Sandberg seems to me to be an idealistic Artemis with rational Athena on her intellectual flank.

I went from being barely acquainted with Hestia to realizing that this is the archetype that provides a center/home base for my inner and outer life. This was an after-fifty shift for me. I was surprised to find how much I loved living alone and that I am nourished by the solitude and serenity of my home. I go from being Hestia into my work-and-friendship world, and then into the larger world when I travel. I do my creative work and the networking that activism requires within this Hestia space of home and psyche. It's a subtle energy thing, being with this archetype, which differs from the other two. Staying focused is a quality of consciousness that Artemis and Athena have in common. Not so for Hestia. And yet *focus* is the Latin word for "hearth," which is where Hestia can be found.

Hestia represents a centering focus, a spiritual center around which the activities of my inner and outer lives revolve. I appreciate having activated virgin-goddess archetypes; they make living fun and meaningful. Artemis motivates or energizes me to do what matters to me and keeps me on a heart path; Athena figures out how best to accomplish these things, and watches over resources so I don't overspend myself in the time-energy column. Hestia is restorative on a daily basis, providing enough quiet in my psyche and surroundings when I am awake, and giving me restful sleep. In this mostly virgin-goddess terrain, Aphrodite adds presence as well—I see and feel and walk in beauty, which is to feel blessed. It's such an energy arc!

As I meet women who are drawn to non profits and activist causes, I find that many younger women have one foot in the very real world where there are big problems, while the other is rooted spiritually in a melting pot of eclectic beliefs that is their source of energy and conviction about what is important to them. I find that many women in their fifties, sixties, and seventies are in transition. They may be empty-nesters seeking new sources of meaning, facing retirement, or finding themselves with new energy for relationships or creativity. I hear about widowed mothers of friends who fulfilled the traditional role of wife to patriarchal men, who are living alone in active retirement communities, surprised to be in the happiest period of their lives. Some are activists; some are expressing themselves through an artistic medium; some are reading and discussing ideas or going to college classes for retirees. Other than the physical limitations of their aging bodies, they are exercising more sovereign rights than ever in their lifetime. They are choosing how to spend their time and energy—just as privileged young people can do as they enter their adult years.

Chapter Eight

GODDESSES OF THE MOON: ARTEMIS/SELENE/HECATE

Artemis is one of the three Greek goddesses of the moon, along with Selene and Hecate. Each represents a phase in life: Artemis symbolizes the waxing, or young and growing, crescent moon; Selene is the full moon; Hecate is the waning crescent moon. The phases of the moon are often seen as reflections of the three phases of women's lives—as maiden, mother, and crone. These are also the three phases of the pre-patriarchal Great Goddess or Triple Goddess, who was worshipped in her three aspects. However, Selene, as the full moon, is full in herself and is not a mother goddess. She symbolizes the reality that maturity and motherhood are not the same, but rather separate aspects of a woman in her prime. Hecate, as the waning moon, is the archetype of the crone, the mysterious one who phases into the dark of the moon.

For millennia, divinity was seen as the Great Mother and earth was sacred. Indigenous humans lived in a sacred world (which they still do). In pre-patriarchal Old Europe, successive waves of invaders imposed powerful male divinities upon the goddess-worshipping people. Female divinities were either diminished or incorporated, becoming consorts or daughters for the new gods. Greek mythology tells about the struggle for power among the gods. Zeus prevailed and established himself as chief god on Mount Olympus. Rape became a common theme. Under the Romans, the mythology remained similar, although many of the names of divinities were changed.

The Western world was pagan and patriarchal; male gods and men ruled. With the ascendency of Christianity under the Roman Emperor Constantine, pagan divinities were replaced by monotheism—by one male god—although Christianity has a mystical Trinity of father, son, and holy spirit, and Catholics venerate the Virgin Mary. In medieval times, rulers claimed they had been given the divine right to rule over others from God. Only men could be priests, because they were created in the image of God. The theologians not only upheld male superiority; but they also maintained for many centuries that men had souls and women did not.

It is relevant to the status of women to learn that, prior to patriarchal religions, humans worshipped the Great Goddess, mother goddesses, and the sacred feminine, although by many different names. The function of men and sperm in procreation was not known. What was known was that all life came through female bodies and that women were embodiments of the goddess in bringing forth new life. Pregnant women became initiates into the mystery and dangers of childbirth, aided by midwives, older women who recognized the stages of labor. The sick also turned to midwives for their knowledge of remedies to ease pain, lower fevers, and heal wounds.

They could see signs of recovery and know when a person was getting close to death. They were respected and possibly feared because of their proximity to the great mysteries of birth and death. These wise women, midwives, and healers, who were the first to be burned at the stake during the Inquisition as witches, expressed the archetype of Hecate.

Where there was reverence for the sacred feminine, the relationship between a woman's cycles and the moon were clear and the stages in women's lives honored. The first menstruation and its cessation were important, and there were rituals to honor the onset of these new stages. Our language still reflects the connection between women and the moon: *mens* means "moon" in Latin. Menstruation, pregnancy, and menopause reflect the three stages of the moon, and the three phases of the Great Goddess as maiden, mother, and crone.

A girl became a maiden when she first began to bleed and came into her "moon time." In North American indigenous traditions, women retreated into the moon lodge with other menstruating women, as women who live together and are exposed to moonlight menstruate at the same time. This was a powerful time for dreams, especially for archetypal rather than personal dreams. Women continued to have their monthly menses, until they became pregnant and nursed a child, after which they resumed menstruation until they either became pregnant again or entered menopause. It was thought that menstrual blood was retained either to make a baby or to make milk. At menopause, when monthly bleeding stopped, it was thought that the blood was retained in the body, this time to make wisdom.

Atalanta, Artemis, and the Moon

Atalanta is a myth about a human woman whose archetype is Artemis, and her story is analogous to the first stage—the waxing crescent moon phase—of an independent woman's life. When Hippomenes brings Aphrodite into the story, Atalanta comes under her influence and a second archetype becomes active in her psyche—as it often does in women who are like her. Until they fall in love, their passion may be for a cause—for animals or the outdoors, or as a competitor with good male friends and even lovers. Atalanta's myth ends either when she loses the race and will marry Hippomenes, or when she is turned into a lioness harnessed forever to the chariot of Cybele. In the lives of real women with the Artemis archetype, however, there are many chapters beyond the end of the race.

I describe characteristic patterns when Artemis remains the dominant archetype and major influence throughout a woman's life in *Goddesses in Everywoman*. However, another or other archetypes often do become important and, when they do and are in conflict with Artemis, anxiety arises over decisions that will alter her life. Usually these involve someone else, another archetype, and a loss of autonomy. It may be a relationship choice about commitment or whether to have a child. It could be about making a career change, taking a creative risk, making a geographic move, or in response to unexpected responsibilities. These are big decisions that set the direction a woman's life will take next.

In the first half of life, the metaphor of the inner committee with a well-functioning ego chairing the process is an excellent model. Inner conflicts occur when there are strong archetypal forces and voices competing within a woman; these can arise over love, an opportunity, or a loss. A competent chair (you—a centered, a well-functioning ego) allows all to be heard. However, important decisions should not be determined by a committee vote. The inner committee may bring up the issues and questions, but which path engages your soul? When Artemis is the archetype, an inner one-in-herself certainty can set a young woman on her course early through a life-shaping soul decision.

Another metaphor from mythology about consciousness and choice starts with the question: Which goddess gets the golden apple marked "For the Fairest?" This question comes up at a wedding banquet to which all of the Olympian divinities are invited except Eris, Goddess of Discord. She comes anyway, and rolls a golden apple into the midst of the guests on which is written "For the Fairest." Three goddesses, each representing one of the three categories in *Goddesses in Everywoman,* claim it is meant for her! Will it go to a virgin goddess and represent goals and focus, a profession, a business, or academic life? Will it go to a vulnerable goddess and represent the desire to be married, to become a wife or mother? Or will it go to the alchemical goddess, the lover and creative woman whose love for beauty, passionate intensity, and immediacy will be decisive? In the myth, Zeus declines to make the decision and passes it on to Paris, a shepherd and a prince of Troy. His choice leads to the Trojan War. Until the Women's Movement, men did the choosing and society's values decided not only what was important, but also what was possible.

Which goddess gets the golden apple? That is the question you must answer when the archetypes in your psyche determine what will be meaningful to you—which may change at different times in your life. Outside influences, including pressure to do what "everybody" does, come into the decision. But the depth of a commitment made and the joy that may come of it in your life depend upon the strength of the archetype, which only you can know.

SELENE—GODDESS OF THE FULL MOON

Selene, Goddess of the Full Moon, is called Luna by the Romans. While Artemis and Hecate are associated with the moon, Selene is *the moon incarnate*. She is a Titan—the generation of Greek divinities that ruled prior to the Olympians. Horse-loving women who already see themselves as following an Artemis pattern will be delighted with the image of Selene, the mature next stage of the moon. She is depicted as a woman riding side-saddle on a horse, or in a chariot drawn by a pair of winged horses. She wears a crown with the lunar sphere or crescent on it, or has these moon images on her cloak. Her full-moon nature is not that of a maiden or a pregnant woman, but that of a *full* woman.

With the description of Selene as the full moon incarnate, I was struck with the realization that it was her fullness *as she is* that needs emphasis. A virgin-goddess woman is one-in-herself. In the maturity of midlife, a woman with Atalanta/Artemis qualities can come into her fullness through her own inherent qualities being brought to maturity, and not as a consequence of pregnancy. Her passions and dedication, her perseverance and development, may result in a body of creative work, a profession, or the maturity of an organization, which she recognizes would not have developed had she had children. She can say: "I am a full woman."

This affirmation of self appears in a healing chant by Rachel Bagby that came to her in a dream that seemed to last all night (hosted at *www.vimeo.com*). In it, women of all ages, colors, sizes, heights, and ethnicity sing and chant: "I am a full woman, I am a full woman" as they dance in circles and in spirals. At the end of the chant, women from all over the world turn to declare their fullness. This dream came to Rachel when she was "feeling anything but full." It was a healing song for her and, since then, has been so for countless other women who dance and chant and take this message to heart.

The Genealogy of Selene

Although Greek mythology is patriarchal, its cosmology—its "in the beginning" story—is very different from that of the monotheistic god of the Old Testament, who created heaven and earth by his word. Hesiod's *Theogony* is a metaphoric telling of the Greek story.

At first there was Chaos, Eros, and Gaia. Chaos was formless and primordial; Eros was an energy that may either have emerged from Chaos or been simultaneously present. *Eros* is the Greek word for "love," for the energy of attraction (from molecules to masses to people) that leads to the creation of something new. At first, this energy was not personified. Much later and down the genealogical line, however, we meet Eros the god, son of Aphrodite, in the story of Eros and Psyche. In his further devolution, Eros has become Cupid, the baby in diapers with the bow and love arrows.

After Chaos and Eros, Gaia (the Earth) took form, becoming matter (from Latin *mater*, for "mother"). She gave birth through parthenogenesis to Uranus (the sky), and then mated with him to bring forth the Titans, the elder divinities that personify elements in nature. Hyperion (God of Light) and Theia (or Thea, meaning simply "goddess") became, in turn, the parents of Selene (the moon), Helios (the sun), and Eos (dawn). Thus the Titan divinities of the sun and moon are brother and sister, the same as Apollo and Artemis.

Very little is said about Selene in myths, other than as genealogy, with one notable exception—the story of Selene's love for the sleeping handsome youth, Endymion, that captivated poets and painters. Keats wrote his epic poem *Endymion,* substituting Cynthia for Selene (Cynthia, like Diana, is another name for Artemis). Tintoretto, Van Dyke, and Rubens all painted the pair with Diana/Artemis in the place of Selene.

Endymion

In the myth, Selene comes upon Endymion as he sleeps in a cave on Mount Latmos and falls in love with him. She kisses him and watches over him as he sleeps. She is so attracted to him that she is absent from the night sky and becomes paler and paler. When Zeus discovers that Endymion is the cause of her strange behavior, he gives him the choice between death in any way he prefers or perpetual sleep together with eternal youth. Endymion chooses the immortality of perpetual sleep and youth in his cave on Mount Latmos, where he is still visited in the night by Selene. In another version, Selene herself is so overwhelmed by his beauty that she puts him into a deep sleep so she can kiss him without his knowledge.

This myth doesn't always come to mind when we say that someone "moons over" another person, but it certainly does describe that state of obsessive longing, which is often accompanied by loss of appetite and getting paler and paler metaphorically. This one-sided state of being in love with someone who does not even know of your existence sounds like a freshman girl with a crush on the high school star, or the swooning fans of the current androgynous singer—which are Aphrodite awakenings in teenagers. Or it sounds like Wolfgang von Goethe's *Sorrows of Young Werther*, the classic German romantic novel of unrequited love. Or it could be Dante, who saw Beatrice only once—an encounter that inspired him to write the *Divine Comedy*. One glimpse of her stirred him deeply and had a profound effect on his creativity.

A woman who finds herself being Selene to an Endymion may go through a phase in which she is deeply enamored, and yet wants the beloved on whom she gazes to remain asleep or unconscious of her passionate fascination. In the myth, Selene goes to the cave on Mount Latmos to gaze upon and kiss Endymion, who remains asleep. By the time a woman who is an Artemis reaches midlife or beyond, energies that may have gone into her connection to nature and animals, into a cause, or into being a competitor can become intensely focused on the beauty of one person whom she sees in her own "moonlight" vision. She may hold the image of this beloved person in the cave—in the privacy of the depth of her heart—because it is not like her, she who never fell in love easily, to be moonstruck over someone.

A woman in a Selene/Endymion situation may be married, may have children, may have advanced in her career and be at a plateau, all of which are elements in her ordinary life. Whatever the outer circumstances, she is entering the full-moon phase of her *inner* life by enacting this myth. It is like an enchantment. She is taken over by the intensity of what she feels and probably does not express this to the person who evokes these feelings—quite possibly because it seems so inappropriate or is a threat to her work, relationships, and sense of identity. The beloved may be a gay man or a far younger man, a public figure, a priest, a spiritual leader, her therapist, her student, her client, her patient, or perhaps a new friend. Her Endymion may be a woman or a man.

In Freudian theory, *libido,* the psychic energy of attraction, can only be sexual—either heterosexual or homosexual. In the depth psychology of Jung, libido includes this, but is more. It is Eros—love, vitality, psychic energy that attracts, transforms, and heals. In the vessel of Jungian analysis, Eros must be present for there to be alchemy. In patriarchy and in the minds of most men, attractions are defined and dismissed as sexual. Jungian theory and analysis, on the other hand, differentiates between "homoerotic" and "homosexual" attractions and relationships. The power of patriarchy and psychology to pathologize and categorize is losing its power as a younger generation accepts that boys and men can have "man crushes" and "bro-mances" that don't define their sexual orientation. Same-sex crushes in young girls on older girls and young teachers was never pathologized, perhaps because they went unnoticed and were mostly about being drawn to something in another girl or woman that was their own growing edge. Projections are often positive, occurring when qualities and abilities that are coming into consciousness are projected onto a role model. We may see the other person in the magical light of who we may become through knowing them.

Endymion Attractions

Patriarchy's assumption of male phallic sexual superiority, together with the inferior status of women, made virginity—followed by sexual exclusivity, bearing children, and maintaining a household—what was expected of women and what matters. Men did the choosing. This underlies the traditional form of marriage, which is still the norm. In egalitarian marriages, both members consider themselves equals, friends, and partners. When owning a home and having children, the couple often focuses upon practical issues like communication about schedules and sharing household tasks or children's needs. When both partners focus on work goals and functioning well as a couple, the smoothly running household is not threatened. What may be going on in a woman's head or heart or in relationships with anyone else may be of little consequence for many husbands. It may be his disinterest in a depth connection with her or her own disregard of what her soul thirsts for—which may be spiritual, psychological, aesthetic, creative, or intellectual—that can set the emotional stage for someone to enter her psychic life as an Endymion.

The woman may not reveal her feelings for reasons that have to do with roles, age differences, inhibitions, or her own lack of understanding or misinterpretation of the attraction. How possessed she is by her feelings may be embarrassing to her; to realize the other person isn't attracted to her in the same way or with the same intensity may be humiliating—even if no one else knows any of this. The depth and irrationality of her feelings can make her vulnerable, especially if exposed. When this is the case, like Selene, she may just as soon prefer that the beloved one stay asleep—remain unconscious of how often she goes inside her private world, her inner cave, to be with her Endymion. As a result, she who had been shining so brightly in the outer world may now be drawn into her inner world. She may become moody, introspective, or dissatisfied with the outer world that once captured her attention.

There is something mysterious or mystical about Selene's obsession with Endymion. The word "mysterious" is derived from *mystes*, the name for the initiates into the Eleusinian Mysteries of ancient Greece. These initiates were likely in an altered state. We don't know what their experiences were. But we do know that, as a result of their initiation, they did not fear death. Spiritual transformations, ecstatic epiphanies, and profoundly deep feelings are all beyond the usual or ordinary, but well within human experience. They seem to have in common a mystical dimension of enhanced meaning. When a one-in-herself mature woman becomes obsessed by another person, she may intuitively know that this attraction is about something stirring in her that has been evoked. She may be able to see and describe the person as anyone *not* obsessed would, and yet still feel this other, unreasonable, mysterious attraction. She may be unaccountably emotional and tearful. She may have powerful archetypal dreams. All this may mystify her or be distressing; and yet something in her is now also vividly alive.

Women with Selene as an active archetype should ask themselves: Who is this symbolic, archetypal, mystical someone *as an inner figure*? What yearnings for healing, for wholeness, or for living an authentic life does he or she bring, or touch in them? And who is it in their psyche that is responding?

When a reasonable, mature woman falls in love and is obsessed, her usual ego is unseated as chief executive officer of the psyche by the range and depth and sensitivity of her feelings and by her obsessive thoughts. Even so, she may be able to choose what she does. She is in the grip of emotions and uncertainties that, if shared with significant others—including whoever is her Endymion—may cause outer drama as well. Like other midlife crises, this situation can test everyone involved and shake up assumptions and relationships. A woman whose strong archetypes are the virgin goddesses may grow in depth through this experience. She may gain compassion for others, learn humility, and become connected with feelings and emotions she had walled off in herself.

Mystical Contemplative Passion

Passion is about intensity—not necessarily about a physical drive for sex. Passion plays are, for example, about Jesus Christ. There may be something vaguely familiar about Selene going into the cave each night to gaze adoringly upon sleeping Endymion, whom she kisses without his being aware. It's like a mother who tiptoes into a dimly lit room at night to gaze upon her sleeping child, kissing him or her lightly so as not to disturb sleep, stirred by deeper feelings than she has ever felt for anyone. She may catch her breath in awe and wonder. At that moment, the sleeping child or young adult is a miracle, a divine child.

John Keats' famous first line in his epic poem *Endymion*—"A thing of beauty is a joy forever"—speaks to these precious moments when joy is the response to beauty. These are timeless, forever moments, totally out of ordinary time. A Selene/Endymion attraction begins in the soul with an "Ahh, how beautiful!" For one-in-herself women, this attraction to beauty—of form or of soul—allies with her own soul's need to love more and love more deeply, which conspires against her independence.

Selene's nightly visit to the mountain cave to gaze at Endymion has qualities of a meditative or contemplative spiritual practice in which a mystical passion for the beloved is at the center of worship. When it is an inner experience, it holds the image in her heart and fills her with feelings for her beloved. This mystical passion for the beloved is what Rumi speaks to in his poems. It may be similar to the ecstatic mysticism of Teresa of Avila, who experienced the rapture of union with God as she prayed in her cell at night. Viktor Frankl could fill himself with bliss by deeply remembering his wife, who was killed along with all of his family in the Nazi concentration camp in which he survived; he did this in the midst of misery and with atrocities all around him. It is a deep active-imagination experience that is real in the invisible world of images imbued with presence.

The myth of Selene brings in a mystical, interior receptivity that can emerge in the psyche when Artemis is an archetype. Just as the Artemis archetype makes sisterhood natural or idealized, the moon aspect of Artemis is the tendency in the archetype to be a contemplative or mystic.

Vulnerability and Attractions

It is heart-opening or heart-deepening to acknowledge loving someone as Selene loved Endymion and then risk not knowing where it will lead. In real life, the "Ahh" moment between two people passes, unless it is held in the soul or cave of the heart. Effort to possess it again leads to longings. And it requires courage of a different kind than that needed to face down a boar to go voluntarily into the cave—the ancient entry into the underworld of the dark feminine—and find your way by moonlight, which is a different way of seeing. In moonlight, the world of nature is mysterious and rich in potential meaning; there is beauty and a felt sense of the original oneness with everything. It is the realm of the poet; in neuroscience, it is right-brain perception.

To feel yourself behaving out of character (even if no one else sees it), to be infatuated, to be vulnerable, to have your sense of well-being dependent on someone else is not a comfortable state. It is uncharted and unfamiliar emotional terrain for independent one-in-herself women, who find themselves in a tension of opposites between their independent old way of being and the intensity of the attraction and what it may represent. Here, psychological reflection is called for. Who—*as if a dream figure*—is this unconscious person who does not know or can not return your feelings? Is there some value to feeling so intensely? For those who think concretely, it can be very hard to see beyond the person to the powerful symbol that may be promising wholeness or healing, which is the real attraction. Selene's attraction to youthful, beautiful, and unconscious Endymion may, then, be more than a compelling fascination for a person; for these women, it may be something more that is missing in themselves.

There are masculine, feminine, and androgynous inner figures that appear in dreams that can shimmer like the iridescent colors on the chest feathers of a hummingbird or kingfisher. They may seem to be intermediaries, guides to numinous contents in the collective unconscious. This is a more comfortable lure than a real person who is really a symbol. But, just as a figure in a dream comes uninvited, a fascinating, magical person in the outer world can unexpectedly show up in your life and become an obsession. A Selene may not want a real relationship with the person who is her Endymion. She is not blind to realities in the outer world that has been familiar terrain. Her inner wisdom knows that she is being drawn into deeper spiritual feelings in her own psyche by his (or her) beauty—which is not just in the eye of the beholder, but is a response in her soul or her subtle heart. When this happens, like Selene, she may not feel a need to wake whoever it is who has the role of Endymion.

When Both Are Awake

When, however, both people in a Selene/Endymion attraction are awake to the existence of a mutual mystical attraction between them, the spiritual tasks are to hold the tension between them and to feel, express, and describe the feelings and images that arise. They must be honest and authentic with themselves and with each other, which means becoming known and vulnerable to the other. They will then be in an individuating relationship that fosters soul growth, compassion, and wholeness. This is hard to do, unless it is important to both and a priority. One or the other may acknowledge the mutuality of attraction, but not want to explore the depth or meaning of it. One or both may be in a committed relationship that this attraction will threaten. And in most people's lives, there are competing demands for time and attention.

When an Atalanta/Artemis woman realizes that she is now Selene and that this relationship is alive in her inner world but is not real in the outer world, she can consciously decide to stay with her feelings anyway. By enduring the mystery and seeking meaning and clarity—through creativity, dreams, synchronicity, or therapy—her subtle heart grows in its capacity to hold and know (*gnosis*). The temptation is to reduce the attraction by claiming that "it's only sexual tension," or "it's only a projection," defining and dismissing the attraction as a trick of the mind or a figment of the imagination. Or perhaps acknowledging and then minimizing it as a soul connection—"maybe a previous life," a just-so story—just the way it is.

In midlife Selene/Endymion attractions, elements of all three are likely present. There is libido—passion that may or may not have a sexual goal; there is an element of projection; and there is likely a soul connection. The attraction can result in friendship or marriage. In some situations, as in depth psychology or spiritual work, the relationship may be limited and defined by ethical boundaries that make expression of feelings safe but acting on them unethical. When so contained, projections and transference can be analyzed and feelings sublimated, which can lead to psychological and spiritual growth.

It would be a mistake to assume that a Selene/Endymion attraction is *only* about the relationship between the two people. This may be similar to the mistake that

Jung described in his letter to Bill W., the founder of Alchoholics Anonymous, of turning to alcoholic spirits when the thirst is really for Spirit and community. The initial high from alcohol or drugs may lead to addiction in place of a spiritual or mystical experience that is the true yearning. The absence of this experience may be the source of pain, just as drugs or alcohol may have initially created a false sense of ease with people when the yearning is for a deep emotional connection to others. Turning to Spirit and to other AA members who are there for each other provides what was missing before the addiction. In Selene/Endymion relationships, the meaning of the attraction is always a puzzle worth understanding, no matter how it ends, whether it ever began, or whether it continues to grow. Being drawn to beauty is a soul response. It can lead to healing and forgiving ourselves and others, as well as bring new depth, even if it takes you through a broken heart—which for Atalanta/Artemis is an initiation into becoming more human and less the archetype.

Hecate—Goddess of the Waning Moon

Hecate, Goddess of the Crossroad and of the Waning Moon, was the third, crone, aspect of the moon. In ancient Greece, Hecate was present where three major roads came together, represented by a statue or pillar with three faces. One face looked down the road that brought the traveler to the crossroad. The other two could see where each of the other two paths would lead. Hecate can see where you are coming from, and what your choices are. This may relate to a decision that will affect the direction your life will take. Or it may be a major inner crossroad, a soul decision.

Hecate wears a gleaming headdress or headband of stars and holds a flaming torch in each hand. She walked the roads of ancient Greece accompanied by her black hounds. In some symbolic representations of Hecate, instead of three faces or heads, she is accompanied by three animal symbols—the dog, the snake, and the lion, or the dog, the horse, and the bear. At her crossroads, usually during the dark of the moon, people left food called "Hecate suppers" as offerings to her. Hecate is a Titan, the only one of this earlier generation of Greek divinities that Zeus greatly honored. She is the sister of Leto, the powerless mother of Artemis and Apollo.

Hecate is a liminal presence. She is found at twilight, between night and day. She is at home in caves, places between the upper world and the underworld, the world of the living and that of the dead or of the spirits. She is the archetype of the medium or psychic, the healer, the midwife, and the witch. Hecate's archetypal three-way vision refers to her intuitive ability to make connections between past, present, and future. Intuition is a perception of patterns—a way of seeing how present circumstance and relationships grew from the past and the direction they may move in the future.

Hecate and Transitions

Hecate presides over times of transition—that in-between time when what you decide (or what happens) determines the direction your life will take. As midwife, she knows the stages of labor, and in particular the stage of transition, the last and most dangerous stage just before delivery.

She also knows the stages of dying and is the archetype of hospice workers. In recognizing the relationship between past, present, and future, Hecate is also the archetype in intuitive therapists and in us—if we learn from experience and grow wiser as we grow older. I used to say that I had to become old enough before I could write about Hecate. When I was old enough and did, she was the inspiration and prod to writing *Goddesses in Older Women: Archetypes in Women Over Fifty* (2001).

Hecate is the third goddess in the story of Demeter and Persephone. She makes only two cameo appearances in this long and famous myth, but they are very significant in understanding this archetype. When Persephone is abducted by Hades into the underworld, her grieving mother Demeter searches everywhere on earth for nine days and nights and can not find her anywhere. Finally, she returns to the meadow where Persephone was last seen. Hecate comes to her and says that she didn't see what happened because she was in her cave, but that she heard Persephone's screams. She is supportive and wise when she says to Demeter: "Let us go to see the god of the sun, he was overhead, he saw what happened, he can tell us." She knows that it is important to seek the truth. She doesn't just feel sympathy for Demeter; she takes compassionate action and stays with her.

Hecate is the supportive friend who says: "I'll go with you to the oncologist about that lump in your breast." Or: "I'll accompany you to the Alcoholics Anonymous or the Al-Anon meeting." Hecate is the wisdom in women who know that denial and wishful thinking harm rather than help when the truth must be faced. She is the archetype in you or your friend that knows this.

The second time Hecate appears in the myth is in a one-line comment toward the very end. After Persephone returns to the upper world and is reunited with her mother, Hecate greets her and, as we learn, from that day on, "precedes and follows" Persephone. Some translations just say "accompanies." Hecate represents the wisdom we can learn through descents into the metaphoric underworld if we return.

Hecate is a vague, dimly appreciated, and dimly seen goddess who is not paired with a god. Nor is she overpowered in her mythology. When classical myths describe the Olympian goddesses in triads, Hecate is the crone in all of them. Persephone is the maiden, Demeter the mother, and Hecate the crone; Hebe is the cupbearer and maiden, Hera the wife, and Hecate the crone. Artemis the waxing moon, Selene the full moon, and Hecate the waning moon who passes into that mysterious phase, the dark of the moon.

Usually, Hecate is the archetype of the wise woman/crone who comes into prominence in a woman's psyche in the third, post-menopausal phase of life, which used to be around fifty. As fifty becomes what thirty-five used to be, the middle active years stretch out after menopause for many women. As women live longer, they develop more than their one dominant archetype and spend more years in active middle life as older mothers or in careers. They may reinvent themselves and start new relationships, entering new areas of education, work, or creativity. Hecate can be an inner companion or the major archetype when growing older means growing wiser.

Hecate in her cave differs from Hecate at the crossroad. Her cave is a threshold or entryway into the underworld.

This is a threshold between the space/time outer world, where people agree on what reality is, and the non-ordinary reality of a spirit world. In Greek cosmology, the underworld is not a hell, but rather a place where occasional visitors can see and communicate with the "shades of the dead." In this manifestation of Hecate, a woman is a medium or psychic between these worlds. Many quite ordinary people have had paranormal experiences that I am beginning to think are quite ordinary and usually comforting. They have sensed the presence of someone who was close in life—a parent, spouse, or child, or someone who loved them—someone whose presence after physical death feels like that of a guardian spirit or angel. Some see spirit forms that sound similar to what Odysseus saw when he went to the underworld to seek counsel from Tiresias, the blind seer in *The Odyssey*. He could recognize individuals, but they had no physical substance. If you go to Disneyland and see holograms of people in the Haunted House, you can see right through them and yet the details of their features and clothes are distinct, much as the shades of the underworld could be.

Hecate develops early when there are no trustworthy adults around or when a young girl has no one to turn to for protection much of the time. Atalanta has to find her way by observation, learning from experience what to pay attention to as she makes her way through uncharted forests—a hunter/gatherer who could become prey for a large predator. She is responsible for her own safety; she has to develop and trust her instincts. She often needs to pause and think through what direction to take, to take stock. And over and over, she has to make decisions about where to go and what to do next. A girl on her own in the city who makes her way through city schools and streets also has to make decisions continually about what routes to take, where to go, and whom to trust. When youngsters are on their own, Hecate can become an inner companion early in life. A child who is not looked after by adults learns to stay observant—to learn by watching, to avoid drawing attention to herself, and to learn from mistakes. To become *wise beyond her years*, or to become street-wise, is to develop the Hecate wisdom of seeing patterns and consequences, and seeing into character and soul qualities.

Artemis Growing Older

Onnolee Stevens, still called Onzie although now in her mid-eighties, amazes people when they learn that she goes wilderness camping by herself in a camper truck with only her "sweet dog" as her companion. She got a camper when pitching her own tent got to be too hard on her knees, both of which are now bionic thanks to knee-replacement surgery. She took up tent camping only when she could no longer carry everything she needed on her back. Before that, she used to go backpacking by herself. She backpacked alone across the Inca Trail from Cusco to Machu Picchu in Peru, hiked into the wilderness of eastern Belize, and into the mountains of Communist Yugoslavia. Onzie's love of the wilderness and of being on her own in it are Artemis qualities that other goddess archetypes don't share.

When I asked Onzie how old she was when she first went backpacking by herself, I was surprised when she said she had begun at fifty-five, after divorcing her husband—going into the wilderness alone hadn't fit with a long marriage and eight children. Onzie has a degree in social work, was a therapist, founded non profits, taught and led workshops, and was politically active in causes and for candidates concerned with social justice and women issues. She remains in touch with her grown children and adult grandchildren via email and visits.

After years of being comfortably single, Onzie fell in love and married a second time. She and her husband actively partnered in their work for several years. When they divorced, Onzie moved to a new community to live close to the elements in nature that she most loves—water, sky, and trees. Finally, she settled there. She remains on friendly terms with both former husbands—something Artemis women tend to do, at least after a time. Her most recent work was to follow an intensive hospice training which is, of course, very much a Hecate calling—to work in the liminal time between life and death.

In *The Feminine Mystique* (1963), which along with the report about job inequality from President John F. Kennedy's Commission on the Status of Women (1963) laid the groundwork for the Women's Movement, Betty Friedan wrote about Onzie's generation of women. They had gone to college, married, had children, and were supposed to have everything they needed to be happy by living through their husbands and children in the suburbs. Women were expected to live out the archetypes of the wife and mother and were idealized when they did. Friedan wrote about women who had it all according to role expectations, but who suffered from "the problem with no name"—their unhappiness, compounded by the certainty that they should be happy.

When marriages ended for this generation, divorced women were in a social wilderness where each had to make her way. With the indomitable spirit of Artemis, these women could follow their inner compasses as they set out to answer the question: What now? At first, they often knew only which direction to take. Then, as if on a trail that is criss-crossed by other trails, they found they had to decide time and time again which path to take. Each choice was a Hecate moment, each step a reaffirmation—an everyday decision to stay on their own course, one that could take them farther away from what other people in their lives wanted for them. When you exercise your autonomy and are on a self-chosen path, a life that is meaningful to you becomes possible. But you also run the risk of becoming lost or discouraged as you are finding your way.

Your story may feel like Ayla's, the protagonist in *The Clan of the Cave Bear* (1980), and in subsequent novels by Jean Auel in which Ayla ventures out to find people like herself. This is what goes on in a newly single woman who sets out on her own. How long a journey and how difficult will it be? Can she move on? Will she find support to be herself? Will she find what her heart desires?

For women whose inner lives have been nourished by ideas and stories, there are many possibilities: Go to a lecture with a subject that intrigues you. Check out organizations with principles similar to your own. Sign up for an adventure. Travel to help others or go on a pilgrimage. Go on a trek. Move to where the beauty and changes in the natural world feed your soul. Reach out to old friends in other parts of the country and the world with whom you once had a heart-connection. Choose to stay home with yourself as good company or with a good book, and say no to social invitations that will drain you.

When you are expected to play a role, which is the understanding when you accept some invitations, it takes energy. This is in contrast to authentic meetings between individuals who have a heart or soul connection, who are *real* to each other. In such good company, energy is generated not consumed; you feel more centered, true to yourself; you feel more love. This can happen between two people or in circles with a sacred center that support the individuals in them to share what deeply matters. These circles nurture creativity and heart-activism. Some circles with a spiritual center support projects that make a difference. The configuration of a circle with a center is that of the mandala, the geometric form that C. G. Jung calls a symbol of the Self.

Onzie was a convener of the Millionth Circle initiative, a women's circle that began in 2001 that has a bigger mission, in addition to supporting the lives of the women in it. A circle of women with a sacred or spiritual center like this one supports and witnesses its members—we stay in contact via a monthly conference call and group emails that keep us aware of each others' "lives in progress." We hold a retreat—or Deepening Gathering, as we call it—once a year when we meet face to face in circle. Women who want to be together share the sister archetype of Artemis and, in this circle, Hestia and Hecate are archetypes held in common as well. This is especially so for those of us who live alone. The majority of members are married, with husbands who—like Meleager or Hippomenes—value their wives' competency and support their participation in circles of women.

When Onzie left the mainstream pattern for women of her age, she became an outlier, a now-positive designation for being on the edge rather than in the mainstream. Times have changed since Onzie was in her fifties. When the boomers, the Millennials, and those in between enter their eighties, most will have been at the crossroad with Hecate many times and thereby have lived many "lifetimes," with each major change another "incarnation." Each time, the choice may have been between the broad road of conventional expectations or the trail that takes the direction of personal authenticity. Authenticity rather than conformity has become a cultural value, which was not always the case.

When Onzie first moved to Port Townsend, she knew no one. Having a sense of place, however, she saw an announcement of a Native American event that was open to the public and she decided to go to it. When she arrived and looked around, she found she was the only white person there. She was warmly welcomed. This is a culture in which "grandmother" is a title of respect, where the wisdom of older women is welcomed and even a white-haired, older, white woman then in her late seventies who came on her own was treated as an honored guest.

This tradition of valuing the grandmothers was embedded in the governance of the Iroquois Confederacy, also called the Seneca Nations. This culture trusted the collective wisdom of the council of women elders to decide the priorities for the people, including whether to go to war. They, in effect, honored the wisdom of Hecate, of women beyond the age of childbearing whose own children were now adults. Their concern was for the well-being of all the children of the six tribes. Like Hecate, they were expected to see three ways: into the past, into the present, and into the future. They weighed the likely effect of their decisions upon seven generations to come.

In 2004, a group indigenous grandmothers from around the world were brought together. They met in circle and became the Council of the Thirteen Indigenous Grandmothers. Each was, in age and wisdom, an embodiment of Hecate. As individuals, each had precognitive experiences—mediumistic, psychic, intuitive foreknowledge—that they would someday have this role, even though it was unimaginable logically. Together and individually, they pay attention to the visible and invisible worlds. They easily inhabit the liminal threshold between these worlds. They may have appeared different from one another when they were young, as the ancient Greek goddesses seemed in their earlier aspects, but their final common pathway was Hecate. As they are honored and invited to meet with leaders and be present at peace conferences, the Thirteen represent wisdom from the sacred feminine, from the indigenous spirituality that recognizes humans as two-legged members of a world in which all forms of life are part of a totality imbued with spirit.

Humanity is at the crossroad with Hecate, because we have consciousness and choice and are at a time when climate change and weapons of mass destruction threaten to turn this beautiful planet into a wasteland. The beauty and ongoing life of the planet comes from Mother Nature's bounty of mountains, forests, oceans, lakes, and wildlife that—from microbe to honey bee, salmon to polar bear and wolf, earthworm to eagle—lives instinctively and unconsciously in ecological interdependence. Wilderness beauty is sacred to Artemis. This is her landscape. To honor her requires taking care of the planet and halting the excesses—from over-population to over-fishing the ocean. We must limit our excesses as a sacrifice to honor the sacred feminine.

It was the failure of the king to honor or sacrifice to Artemis that brought the Calydon boar down on his realm. I think of the boar as a metaphor for the destructiveness of nature—which is indiscriminate. Whatever or whoever is in the path of an avalanche, a flood, a wildfire, a tornado, or a tsunami knows this all too well. These calamities of nature are becoming increasingly common as a consequence of climate change, which is our own Calydon boar. If the king, a symbol of patriarchy, had honored nature and made sacrifices, the boar would not have ravaged his realm. The boar was stopped by Atalanta's arrow and Meleager's sword. One of these mythic figures represents women with the indomitable spirit of Artemis, who can confront danger clearly and close up, hold their ground, take aim at the vulnerable spot, and let the point they are making hit the target. One represents men like Meleager, whose sword symbolizes the power and discernment to act decisively in concert with an empowered feminine in women and in themselves. We need to take aim at the causes of our own destruction—climate change, weapons of mass destruction, war—and then follow up with strong decisive actions.

Chapter Nine

FREE TO BE YOU AND ME

Marlo Thomas begins the thirty-fifth anniversary edition of *Free to Be . . . You and Me* with "Dear You." She says: "You'll also notice that, even though the characters in this book have names that are different from yours, they're really all about you. *Free to Be . . . You and Me* was written to remind you that you are the hero of your own life adventure, and that you can write your story any way that you dream it can be." It warms my heart to think that many young readers may have taken these words to heart and that they may now as members of the millennial generation (born between 1980–1995) be contributing to a "free to be" world.

The message of *Free to Be . . . You and Me* also fits the intention of this book. Myths and stories come most alive when there is a corresponding active archetype in us. Archetypes are patterns, innate ways of being and responding—some more instinctual than others—that are in the collective unconscious. The indomitable spirit that I associate with the Artemis archetype may be apparent practically from birth. In others, Artemis remains latent and may emerge much later in life, or not at all. All archetypes are potentials, any one of which may, for a time, be very important and underlie a phase of life. Archetypes are a way of seeing the "lay of the land," the psychological geography of a person. There will be characteristics in common with others with the same archetype, but each person is a unique and special variation of it.

This life we have, with its twists and turns, is our story to shape and find meaning in. *Enthusiasm* and *vitality* are signs that we are living the life we were meant to live or are being who we were meant to be. When this is not so, there may be emotional numbness, a pervasive sadness, anxiety, and various bodily pains from tensions and stress—all of which can happen when we put on a persona or social face and identify with a role, acting as if we enjoy and want to be in the life we have. Taking a pill for what ails us may make us more comfortable, but this doesn't bring us a sense of authenticity and spontaneity, which becoming real does. *Real,* as I define it, has to do with soul—soul work and soul connections, terms I use interchangeably with heart work and heart connections. This is not logical (*logos*) knowledge; this is *gnosis*—intuitively felt knowledge. When you are doing soul-satisfying or heart-centered work, you *know* it; when you have a soul or heart connection with another person, you *know* it.

Some things, some people, and some places resonate deeply with an archetype within us. To be able to make choices based upon soul, heart, and archetype gives us a passion for life and a life that is personally meaningful. This is possible only when we are "free to be you and me" and have opportunities and the freedom to choose a soul path. Trust that we *know* when a path is right for us grows as we travel it, because we come to love what we are doing and who we are becoming. This expands consciousness and makes us more receptive to beauty and to feeling part of something larger and ineffable.

Whether it is possible to follow a strong intuition that *this* is the direction to go toward, or that *this* calling or love is right for us, requires freedom to choose. When we are at a crossroad and must decide which direction to take, or are in a transition or liminal phase where there are no defining landmarks, we are in migration. Moving toward what? Often, we don't know where we are going, but know that it *feels* right. Even when we set out to cover a known number of miles—as Cheryl Strayed did when she started to walk the Pacific Crest Trail, or as Elizabeth Danu did when she set out to bicycle from Seattle to San Diego—reaching the destination becomes almost incidental compared to the experience.

Perpetual Migration

In her poem "The Perpetual Migration" (*The Moon is Always Female*, 1980), Marge Piercy writes with a poet's ambiguity when she refers to "we:"

How do we know where we are going?
How do we know where we are headed
till we in fact or hope or hunch
arrive? You can only criticize,
the comfortable say, you don't know
what you want. Ah, but we do.

Is she speaking about you and me? About women? About humanity? Or, as it seems to me, about all of the above? When she asks how we know where we are going, I think of the instinctive migrations of birds and fish, of sprouting seeds that grow upward toward the sunlight. I think that humankind is on an evolutionary journey, which is our migration. And each of us participates in where we are going. In my profession, I see how individuals thrive when they can make meaningful choices and when their individual gifts are encouraged to develop. I see how fear inhibits and how love expands consciousness. I see that consciousness involves intellect, heart, and soul. I see how people change and evolve to become more spiritual and compassionate. I see them realize when they are in narcissistic codependent relationships, and I see them use this insight to change their behavior—which allows them to change the relationship or choose to leave it. I speculate that what is true for individuals may be coming true for humanity. Perhaps this is why democracy is a rallying movement in countries that have been ruled by despots. Or why the news is full of incidents in which ordinary people, including women, are taking to the streets in protest and celebration.

Each of us thinks of ourselves as a separate entity and yet, as members of humanity, we are traveling together with our species. Our individual psyches echo themes in the collective—egalitarian and patriarchal, expansive and regressive, fearful and loving. We move through historical time in much the same way as immense schools of small fish move through the sea or as huge flocks of birds in migration fill the skies. In this collective of over seven billion human beings, the archetype of Artemis is being liberated through individual women. Feminism, equality between men and women, sisterhood, circle rather than hierarchy are ideas with the power to transform individuals, who in turn shift the direction of collective humanity through the effects of being in the human morphic field, influenced by changes in the collective unconscious as well as by conscious thought and action.

Those with an active Artemis archetype come into the world with self-determination, a strong will, and the ability to focus. This likely also comes with a sense of fairness, an egalitarian attitude, and a protective emotional response toward weaker others who can't protect themselves. A girl had better hide these qualities and values if she grows up in circumstances where she must be obedient, seen and not heard. A boy with a strong will, self-determination, and focus may be praised for these qualities, but wherever domination is equated with masculinity, boys with an innate sense of equality, fairness, and protectiveness may hide it in order to be "one of the boys" and a man among men. In either situation, that which is unacceptable and labeled as unfeminine or unmasculine goes underground, where it can become a source of feeling badly about ourselves. But if a child is wise—and many are—he or she learns from observing and is realistically cautious about expressing this part of herself or himself. The indomitable spirit in them, while not exposed and expressed, may be supported to grow in the imagination by stories and myths—and now also by news and ideas that reach them through the Internet.

The Toxicity of Power

Joy emerges with freedom because, when there is freedom to be creative and expressive, there is joy. When power dominates the psyche, the family, or the halls of patriarchy, there is a notable lack of joy, because power goes hand in hand with fear. Fear inhibits laughter, spontaneity, and creativity; it squelches the inner child and is not concerned about what is best for children, the country, or the planet. Where power and intimidation rule, paranoia is adaptive. Inner peace in such psyches or households or institutions is absent. Walking as if on eggshells, so as not to set off explosive anger or punitive action, is adaptive. Wherever violence is a reality or power has the last word, joy is missing.

In contrast, when you are free to be yourself, joy is a significant element in your life. Watch a child do something on her own that takes effort. For example, when a little Atalanta takes her first steps *on her own*—she beams at the accomplishment and wants to do more of this. She does not need an audience to encourage her or to hover over her in case she falls and hurts herself. She will fall; she will pick herself up; and she will stick with it until she can walk—and then run. One day, she'll put this same effort into climbing a tree or achieving a goal; she will fall and pick herself up, and keep at it until it's done. Later in life, that same determination may make her persevere in her activism or her work. She may be an athlete that strives for her personal best or a competitor who wants to be the best. She may work at something until it is done to her own deep satisfaction. These are moments of achieving or creating something that has internal value. It doesn't matter if there is anyone else to see what she has done, or anyone who understands the big smile on her face. There is inner joy at having done it. Appreciation from others, applause, rewards—these are secondary satisfactions that may come later.

When perseverance and focus are built-in traits, an Atalanta/Artemis is hard to distract when she's intent on what she is absorbed in doing, or when she has strong feelings—which are likely to be about limits on her autonomy or something she protests as *not fair!* It seems that such a girl comes into the world ready to declare her sovereignty—a word usually applied to a nation that means autonomy, independence, liberty, self-determination, self-governance, and freedom.

These are qualities that are not welcomed in girls and women in households within patriarchal cultures, however, or in those with a controlling parent. Punishment and judgments, abuse and restrictions teach these girls that they are not *free to be* who they really are. Efforts may be directed at breaking their spirit if they persist. With perseverance and the ability to aim for a distant target when it is possible, however, girls raised in families that are oppressive may decide to bide their time until they can leave home at eighteen to express their sovereignty.

While parents and society may support or suppress some archetypes and encourage others—whether welcomed or not if a girl starts life with a strong streak of Artemis in her psyche—these are attributes that she has and that they react to. Daughters with indomitable spirit come from a variety of families. In my practice and awareness, their fathers and mothers vary. They may have been raised into adulthood in an intact nuclear family, or one parent may have died when they were young. Their mothers may be professionals or corporate executives, or may work for other women as domestics or be full-time homemakers; they may be single mothers, or disabled by depression or mental or physically illness. Their fathers may have been benign, indifferent, involved, or distant; they may have been loving or abusive and susceptible to rages made worse by drinking. They may have been successful Zeus figures whose daughters are the apple of their eye; or they may have molested or raped their daughters, or demeaned and abused them. They may have been world famous, or failures in their own eyes and the eyes of the world. They may have been eternal hippies. Their daughters may have been latch-key kids.

In short, there is no family constellation that creates daughters with indomitable spirit. It is an archetypal attribute that includes being "one-in-herself." Efforts to "break their spirit," as one might a spirited horse, may or may not succeed—as can killing them. Or they may become convinced that this archetype makes them bad, unworthy, and unfeminine, and turn on it themselves. In this case, these daughters become ashamed of the Artemis qualities that would otherwise be a source of authenticity and meaning for them.

Procrustes and His Bed

In mythic times, travelers on the road to Athens had to pass Procrustes and his bed. I think of Athens as a symbolic destination, and all of us as travelers who experience lying on his infamous bed. If you were too tall for the bed, one "whack" and you were cut down to size to fit it. If you were too short for the bed, you would be stretched, as on a medieval torturer's rack, until you fit. "Procrustean" has come to mean conformity to expectations which are often arbitrary.

Athens was a center of power and of culture. It stood for collective goals and expectations. Encountering Procrustes on the "road to Athens" is thus a story about social acceptability, gender expectations, and conformity—the many hoops we must jump through to impress others, to get into schools from pre-Kindergarten on, to be hired, to become engaged and married, to be invited where we want to go. We are put on this Procrustean bed over and over; it is what shapes what others see about us and determines how they judge us. In order to be accepted, we suppress qualities of which family, religion, society, peers, potential mates, or spouses disapprove in order to fit their expectations.

In this Procrustean process, qualities that are considered attractive and acceptable can often be "stretched thin," especially when we identify with our *personas*—the image we show others named for the tragedy and comedy masks worn by actors in ancient Greece—and do not acknowledge that there is more to us than how we appear. Procrustean-bed adaptations and conformity to expectations—where possible—support self-esteem, the acquisition of an education and a spouse, and entry into the adult world of work. These adaptations are often not personal enough or deep enough, however, until archetype and life come together.

Midlife crises are often initiated from Procrustean "amputations"—the suppressed and denied parts of our personality that were unacceptable. That which is cut off often remains alive in the unconscious, to be projected onto others, who then attract or repel us. Sometimes we turn to addictions to numb these feelings, but this may instead only loosen our control of them. It is only in the second half, or even the last third, of life that our individuality and creativity may emerge—sometimes out of the ashes of our former life

Finding Your Song and Singing It

Midlife is a time when we take stock of where we are in life; we become aware of how quickly time has passed and that it is altogether possible that the number of years left to us are equal to or less than those we have lived so far. In Jungian psychology, this is the time for inner work, which involves, in part, going into the underworld to retrieve and "re-member" those parts of us lost in the Procrustean process. In Jungian analysis, "individuation" is important; its goal is to become genuine, not perfect, and to be as aware as we can be of what is acting on us and in us. *Free to Be . . . You and Me* envisioned a land where girls and boys could grow up to be who they were meant to be. This is pretty much the hoped-for outcome in Jungian work as well. Archetypes are important sources of meaning, but they may also be embedded in emotional complexes that can take us over. In this work, soul questions arise; image and essence may be in conflict. We may have to bear the tension of holding opposites, or take a big step without knowing where it will lead. Loyalty to others may conflict with responsibility for our own soul growth, holding us in a tension of opposites until a solution emerges that transcends the either/or dichotomy of logic.

Joseph Campbell said that the point is to find and live your personal myth. When asked how to do this, he answered with a question: "What gives your life a sense of harmony and bliss?" Or, as more poetically said by Lawrence LeShan, author of *Cancer as a Turning Point* (1994), the point is to find your song and sing it. LeShan's specific questions for his patients are applicable to us all:

> *What are your special and unique ways of being, relating, and creating that are your own and natural ways to live?*
>
> *What is your music to beat out in life, your unique song to sing so that when you are singing it, you are glad to get up the morning and glad to go to bed at night, tired after a day well spent?*
>
> *What style of life would give you zest, enthusiasm, involvement?*

LeShan worked with terminal patients who were expected to die. Whatever treatments they had gone through—surgery, radiation, chemotherapy—had taken its toll and had not been effective. His questions required that his patients go back into past memory—to a time before the cancer, to childhood, to adolescence, to college, to previous phases of life, to times when they remembered being absorbed and happy. He encouraged them to remember what they were doing that was cut out of their lives and bring it back. Many did—and, as a result, over half went into long-term remission.

Then there is my definition of an "assignment," which is what I have been calling my advocacy for a UN Fifth World Conference on Women (5WCW). The impetus behind this is my conviction that this is a means of energizing a global Women's Movement—a means to accelerate reaching the metaphoric "millionth circle," the women's circle with a sacred center that, added to all the rest, becomes the tipping point that ends patriarchy. An assignment is something you volunteer for. It's something that feels as if it has your name on it. Something that asks questions only you can answer. Is it meaningful? Will it be fun? Is it motivated by love?

Grassroots Feminism

Historical gains made by women, beginning with suffrage, demonstrate a principle that research strongly validates. Women gain rights in a world where power is held mostly by men only when those at the top are motivated by feminist movements that come from the bottom up. We find a recent example of this in India. Only when women took to the streets to protest police disregard of rape was the political will generated to make and enforce laws to protect women. Mala Htun, of the University of New Mexico, and S. Laurel Weldon, of Purdue University, did a depth study of four decades of data collected in seventy countries (1975–2005). They found that it was grassroots feminist movements—not liberal politics, not women's representation in government, not national wealth—that made a difference (*American Political Science Review*, 2012). The study concluded that only strong feminist movements are able to voice and organize around their top priorities as women. In other instances, women are sidelined or subordinated to men's needs or the priorities of institutions or political parties.

It is time to recognize that the alpha males on top of pyramids of institutional, political, and corporate power and wealth are not best-suited to make decisions for humanity and the planet. They determine whether weapons of mass destruction will be developed and used; they seek to control the world's natural resources; they want to own water sources and control food supplies. And they may have sophisticated means to do these things. But if maintaining their power is their major motivation, they are nothing more than warlords or ganglords driven by adrenaline, testosterone, and the need to control property, women, and children.

We know from research at UCLA that women react to stress differently than men do. Women have a "tend and befriend" oxytocin response that is enhanced by estrogen; men have a "fight or flight" response, an adrenaline response that is enhanced by testosterone (Taylor, et. al., 2000). Collaborative agreements, the ability to compromise, the instinct to care for those who are vulnerable, an awareness of the ego needs of powerful men, and the ability to read emotional cues are skills that women, as a gender, have. We can see one example in the twenty women members of the United States Senate who worked out a bipartisan agreement and prevented a second government shut-down. *Time* magazine referred to them as "The Last Politicians" and said they were "looking like the only adults left in Washington" (October 28, 2013).

Women have more connections between right and left brain hemispheres; they have more symmetrical brains than alpha males. Women look for solutions beyond either/or, which is a left-brain dominant limitation. They multi-task, listen to stories, feel as well as think, collaborate, look after children. With education, equality, and empowerment, women are now developing and fine-tuning left-brain wiring. As a result, they have more symmetrical brains than men. Nurturing, creative men have this chracteristic as well; it is apparent in many gay men and men who have taken the opportunity to bond with their children and share work and life schedules with their wives. Men who have been directly influenced by the Women's Movement through their mothers and egalitarian fathers are different; they are "more whole" people than traditional male-identified men. In psychological terms, agency and affiliation are strengths encouraged in both women and men; in Jungian terms, it's the contra-sexual qualities of anima and animus development. Through cultural diffusion, whatever develops in America becomes an influence that is emulated or resisted around the world.

The Girl with No Name

In what can only be called auspicious or synchronistic, I took a break from working on the end of this book to see what my friend, Patricia Smith, was up to. I found her engrossed in a new book, an amazing story of a feral girl who was raised by monkeys (*The Girl with No Name,* Marina Chapman, 2013). The girl was not quite five years old—she recalls that she was looking forward to her fifth birthday—when she was kidnapped from the vegetable garden near her home, most likely in Colombia, South America. She was probably chloroformed. She woke up and went back to sleep hearing the cries of other children. She was aware of being bounced about in a truck, then of being carried over the shoulders of a big man who was rushing or fleeing through the jungle. Then he dropped and abandoned her, and she was on her own in the wilderness.

When she was probably around ten years old, the girl was found by people who showed her far less "humanity" than the troop of Capuchin monkeys that had accepted her. In fact, the rest of her story is more harrowing than the time she spent in the jungle. She obviously did survive, for there is a story to tell, thanks to what she eventually told and taught her daughters—one of whom, Vanessa James, brought the story to print with the professional help of Lynn Barrett-Lee.

Abandoned in a tropical jungle and on her own, the girl with no name was hungry and thirsty—a scared four-going-on-five-year-old. She was surrounded by huge trees, with some sunlight filtering through to the forest floor. There were the sounds of birds and animals, creepy-crawlies, vines and flowers. It was a major stroke of luck that she found herself in the territory of an extended clan of monkeys, most likely Capuchin monkeys, that were smaller in size than she was and not aggressive toward her. They were curious, but not dangerous.

For a long time, the monkeys kept their distance, until the girl ate something that poisoned her and the grandpa monkey acted to save her life. After this, she became one of them. From the beginning, she watched them and ate whatever they ate—because she had learned the hard way that some berries or fruits can be pretty but poisonous. She drank from streams, and urinated and defecated as they did. She was barefoot to begin with and the dress she wore fell apart, leaving her naked, though her hair kept growing. When hunters found her, her hair had grown to cover her torso. By this time, she was a feral child of about ten who got around on all fours and made sounds like the monkeys.

The girl used intelligence and observation to distinguish one monkey from another. She learned what their sounds meant and practiced them herself until she could communicate. She aspired to climb like the monkeys and did not give up trying. She said: "Day after day, for what may have been several months, I would try to climb the shorter slimmer trees. I fell often—sometimes many times a day, and often far and painfully—but I didn't let my failures deter me." She needed to use her feet as the monkeys did. At some point, she ceased walking on two legs and got around on all fours. She wanted to reach the forest canopy, where the sun was warmer and there were some good things to eat. After much perseverance, she did.

When hunters found her, Marina (as she came to be called later) was brought back to a civilization that was more dangerous and cruel than the wild jungle. The hunters sold her to a brothel owner. She was harshly cleaned and trained to behave as human children did. She was used as a domestic slave and kept as a prisoner. She escaped through her own efforts, lucky timing, and an accident of fate. To get away from a customer willing to pay to take her virginity, she hid in an automobile that left the brothel with two other prostitutes and a driver; she was the only survivor when the car was involved in a fatal crash. She was probably about eleven or twelve years old by then, but seemed younger because she was such a small girl—probably due to the jungle diet of mostly fruits, some nuts, and hardly any protein.

In the next two to three years, Marina became a street child who survived by her wits and by stealing. She formed a little gang, and what she saw happening to little ones, even babies, outraged her. She wrote: "I felt such powerful anger for these children. I was so young, and I knew little of the circumstances of these mothers, but my rage for their infants was intense." These feelings for vulnerable, young others and her sense that this was so unfair—the injustice that she encountered and the expectation that it should be otherwise—are archetypally Artemis.

While other street kids sold drugs and used them, while other girls sold sex, Marina avoided both. Something innate in her was wary of losing her sovereignty; she did not want to be trapped and knew that both drugs and sex would trap her. A convent for orphans took her off the streets. There she had a bed, food, and the company of other children; but the price was the loss of her freedom. She would not exchange her freedom for the security of the convent; so, once again, she used her wits and ability to act instinctively and escape.

She went looking for a job as a domestic; in exchange for a place to sleep and food, she would do any household task. She knocked on many doors, but the doors were closed after one look at her. Then, it seemed as if her luck changed. The door to a big house was opened by a woman who had spoken kindly to her in the park and she gave Marina a job. Once in the house, however, she became a prisoner behind high walls and locked doors; this family turned out to be the local equivalent of the Mafia. One day, the head of the family walked in on her in the kitchen. He was not wearing his trousers and he started to feel up her legs. Rather than freezing, she looked around the kitchen for a weapon. She wrote: "I had the advantage of surprise. He didn't know me, and of course he would expect me to acquiesce. But no one—not even powerful Mr. Santos—was going to rape me. Not when I still had air in my lungs." This was an instinctive one-in-herself Artemis response.

The girl with no name was a true-life Atalanta, which intrigued me. One name she did not claim was "victim." Regardless of the circumstances or the adults around her, she retained a sense of agency and sovereignty. She didn't feel sorry for herself or give up. The idea of giving up on herself was never a consideration. I think that she had a commitment to survive and that, *as a consequence*, Providence moved to help her. As W. H. Murray, who headed the Scottish Himalayan Expedition, said: "The moment one definitely commits oneself, then Providence moves, too. A whole stream of events issues from the decision." I refer to "Providence" as synchroncity. Those who survive a grueling or harrowing journey and live to tell the story are usually resilient and inventive, but they also often tell of a stroke of luck, a miracle, or an uncanny coincidence that saved them.

The girl with no name had the good fortune to be abandoned in the vicinity of Capuchin monkeys, rather than in the midst of predators or other primates that live in this jungle. In *The Age of Empathy* by Frans de Waal (2008), the world's foremost primologist, I learned that Capuchins are extremely smart. They have the largest brain relative to body size of all monkeys; they share food and cooperate easily with one another as well as with humans. They are small, cute monkeys, and their chattering kept Marina from feeling alone. Children who are in the natural world are drawn to what they see and can be absorbed and fascinated by it, as this girl was. The monkeys did not hurt her; they were company for her. When she gained their acceptance, she shared in the grooming of frequent touch, which monkeys do with each other. The Artemis/Atalanta in her was *free to be*, because the people or monkeys that were her "kin" had not abused her physically, sexually, or verbally. She had a better childhood, measured by this standard, than many little girls raised in affluence.

One Billion Rising—One Activist's Story

Eve Ensler is the playwright-activist who created *The Vagina Monologues* and One Billion Rising, global demonstrations to stop violence against women. She also wrote a memoir, *In the Body of the World* (2013), in which she tells of her affluent and abusive childhood. Hers is a *much more common* experience than most people are comfortable acknowledging. Her home was in Scarsdale, New York; her father was CEO of a food company, her mother a strikingly attractive, full-time, at-home unmaternal mother. She went to excellent suburban schools and graduated from a private college. Hers is an American picture of a privileged childhood on the surface. On the surface, it doesn't seem as if her story has anything in common with the girl with no name. Beneath the surface, however, she is also a survivor with an indomitable will and courage.

Eve's story begins with the body—her body, a place that she was "forced to evacuate when my father invaded and then violated me." The girl with no name went to sleep with a wary ear—listening for danger, on alert for the sound of animals. Eve and many others with predator fathers do not go to sleep tucked snugly and safely in their beds; they sleep with a wary ear as well, alert for the sound of their fathers' stealthy footsteps in the hall, coming to violate them. When she was older and provoked him (fathers like these look for reasons to be abusive, because raging against a child makes them feel powerful), Eve recalls his ". . . hands choking my throat, [his] fist punching and bloodying my nose."

Eve is a frontline feminist-activist who traveled to over sixty countries to raise awareness and support for abused girls and women. Through her V-Day activism, in which women all over the world perform *The Vagina Monolgues* to raise funds, her work has provided financial support for organizations that work to stop abuse. She did not have an affinity for Mother Nature or trees until she was in the third phase of her life, but her outrage and action on behalf of vulnerable girls and women is a clear expression of the Artemis archetype.

The story of Eve's childhood, her alienation and dissociation from her body (a common result of incest or molestation), and the diagnosis of stage four cancer of the uterus and its treatment came together with the impact of going to the Democratic Republic of the Congo, where she heard and saw the results of the rapes, mutilations, and torture of female bodies from infancy to old age. Her memoir tells of being reunited with her body, and how this united her with the body of the world. Eve writes that, if you are separated from your body, you are separated from the body of the world; everything is connected—oil spills, pillaged earth, rapes. Women activists work to save or protect something they love. It's mother-bear protectiveness on behalf of the vulnerable; it's the archetype shared by women activists. Their causes may differ, but the passion, perseverance, and intensity of their advocacy is an expression of Artemis.

The Girl Who Was Shot by the Taliban

Malala Yousafzai, at fifteen, became the youngest person to be nominated for the Nobel Peace Prize. She was described as a three-year-old who was a delight to her father, Ziauddin Yousafzai, who named her after Malalai, the Afghan Joan of Arc. She went everywhere with him; she was special.

School was the center of Malala's childhood world. Her father was headmaster of the school and the family had an apartment there. Like the pleasure Zeus took in Artemis, Malala's father delighted in his bright daughter, who was eager to learn and could sit absorbed in classes before she was old enough to be enrolled. Once she was a student, she became proficient in languages and fluent in English. Malala's mother was traditional and chose to remain in purdah in public, but she backed her daughter's independence in private.

Malala was eleven years old when the Swat Valley, in the mountainous tribal regions of Pakistan, fell under Taliban rule. Their control finally extended over the entire valley. She was a schoolgirl in Mingora in the lower valley, a vacation destination during the summer months for people from Islamabad, the capital of Pakistan. Sufi music, dance festivals, a nearby UNESCO site of Buddhist art and ruins were attractions. She attended Khushal school for girls, one among 200 that had existed prior to the Taliban. Behind the tall cement walls, Khushal school was an oasis of enlightenment and freedom.

When Malala was twelve, all the girls' schools in the Swat Valley were closed. Her family fled the valley, along with 1.5 million other refugees, when the Taliban took complete control in 2008. They returned when the Pakistan military became a presence in Mingora and the schools reopened. Journalists sought Malala out when they found she could speak so clearly and passionately about what was happening. This led to her blogging under the assumed name of Gul Makai, the heroine of a Pashto folktale. In a widely distributed video, she announced: "I want to serve. I want to serve the people. I want every child to be educated."

In 2012, Malala was returning home from school with friends when an armed gunman, thought to be Taliban, stopped the bus, identified Malala, and shot her in the head and neck. Initially, doctors did not know whether she would live—and if she did live, whether she would be paralyzed. The family moved to England, where multiple surgeries and physical therapy aided her recovery. After several operations, a titanium plate replaces part of her skull, her left jaw and facial nerves have been reconstructed, and a cochlear implant helps her left ear to hear.

Malala's spirit is indomitable. She continues to be an articulate spokesperson, as well as a symbol for the education of girls. On July 12, 2013, Malala addressed the United Nations. In her short and very moving talk, she focused on women's rights and girls' education. Gordon Brown, United Nations Special Envoy for Global Education and former British Prime Minister, launched a petition in Malala's name that led to the ratification of Pakistan's first right-to-education bill in 2013. Her book *I am Malala: The Girl Who Stood Up for Education and Was Shot by the Taliban* was also published in 2013. In her talks and writing, she urges women to stand up for their rights, to fight for independence. She voices the values of Artemis.

MARINA, EVE, AND MALALA

The details of these three narratives have nothing in common. What they do have in common is the indomitable spirit that each of them exemplifies. One woman is a grandmother now; the second is a cancer survivor on the road as an author and activist; the third is a young girl still in her teens with a titanium plate in her head. While Malala is the most famous of the three because she became the youngest nominee for a Nobel Peace Prize, I see Artemis qualities in each of them. But they are all more than the archetype. Like Atalanta, they are all vulnerable mortals.

It took an indomitable spirit, grit, and intelligence for Marina Chapman—a little girl barely five years old—to survive for five years on her own in a tropical jungle by emulating monkeys who gradually accepted her. This part of her childhood resembled Atalanta's mythic beginning, with bear cubs for playmates. It was after she returned to "civilization" that her other Artemis qualities instinctively surfaced—outrage at witnessing babies and young children neglected and treated badly; resisting the loss of autonomy to drug addiction or to a pimp; instinctively fighting off her rapist; leaving a group setting where she could be assured of a bed and food, preferring the freedom she had on the streets to security. Marina's conscious choices and instinctual reactions were expressions of the Artemis archetype. No one taught her to be like this; she had no role models.

The affluent suburban home where Eve Ensler grew up was the site of another remarkable childhood survivor story. Eve couldn't stop the incest and violence that her father inflicted on her. He could physically violate her; but the one-in-herself, virgin-goddess archetype remained intact. She hid this appalling trauma, as children with family secrets do. When she became a playwright and performer, the prohibition against even saying the word "vagina"—and what this meant about how women felt about what was "down there"—was the subject of her consciousness-raising, funny, and poignant *Vagina Monologues.* In her one-woman play, she is the voice for many characters, all of whom talk about, or avoid talking about, vaginas. Her play went on to be performed by women's groups who found in it a bonding and sharing experience; these performances also raised money to help non profits that helped women. Ensler's play is performed by others throughout the United States and beyond on V-Day, creating a ripple effect as more and more performances are done every year. This ripple is on the verge of becoming a tsunami with One Billion Rising, as thousands growing into millions dance in the streets to stop violence against women. Eve is living her personal myth, in which her abusive childhood became an impetus for her creativity and activism. Eve could not stop the violence done to her as a child, but she works to stop it for others and to help victims become survivors.

With One Billion Rising, everyone who participates—the women and men who come out dancing on V-Day to show solidarity and support to stop the violence, the Bollywood stars in India who create songs—is heeding a principle that Gloria Steinem has expressed many times, most recently in a talk just before she received the Presidential Medal of Freedom: "Remember: the end doesn't justify the means; the means *are* the ends. If we want dancing and laughter and friendship and kindness in the future, we must have dancing and laughter and friendship and kindness along the way. That is the small and the big of it" (*Ms.* magazine, Winter/Spring 2014).

Malala Yousafzai, the youngest of these three, was barely out of childhood when she began her mission to advocate for the education of girls. Her intellectual precocity and her fluency in many languages attracted foreign journalists, making her a source of news, but also a target for her enemies. Her resilience in the face of this danger and her fight to regain her health after she was shot made her a symbol of courage and an even more effective advocate for her cause.

There are two powerful synergistic forces shaping Malala into the person she is becoming: the active archetypes in her (Artemis/Athena) and the expectations that others have placed on her (that she is a heroine, that she is special). There is an analogy here to binocular vision, which I introduced in *Goddesses in Everywoman* (1984). We have depth perception because each eye sees the same object from two angles; our brain merges the two images, which provides visual depth. Similarly, two powerful forces act upon us whether we know it or not—the expectations of family and culture (stereotypes) and the archetypes that are active in us. Add to this the historical time and the particular place in which Malala lives—on the literal battleground between fundamentalist patriarchal beliefs and emerging ideas of democracy that lead to equal rights and empowerment of women. This ideological/

psychological conflict is more extreme in Afghanistan than in North America, but the same struggle is taking place here. The United States has not passed the Equal Rights Amendment or ratified CEDAW (Convention Eliminating Discrimination Against Women).

Moreover, there is also something ineffable yet real in everyone that is mystical and spiritual, where personal meaning and free will come in. It's the universally held notion that each of us has a soul; with this comes the sense that we have our own soul's purpose, which has something to do with what we encounter of privilege and suffering, and how we respond.

The Courage of Children

I also see Marina, Eve, and Malala as examples of courageous and competent children. Many people need to remember that they were brave children. So many had to have courage to face real and imagined fears. Children feel afraid and do what is expected of them just the same. By forgetting these times, they also forget the brave children they had to be. For these children, everyday events were fraught with danger, a wilderness of unknowns—each new school, the neighborhood, the walk to school or to the store, coming home not knowing if it had been a good day or a bad one for a parent. These dangers are not usually as bad, objectively, as the dangers of living in an African village in the midst of civil war or having to walk miles to get water or firewood among possible human and animal predators. But for children, their perilous situations are their own personal danger zones. It takes courage and strategy for them to act casually while on hyper-alert, worried that their tormentors may be lying in wait for them after school or that an abusive parent may be on a rampage at home.

I think of the successful adults I know who, as children, had to call on courage daily. In middle school, a boy who didn't even know what gay meant was tormented by another boy and beaten up in front of others who watched. He was an unwilling participant in a spectator sport, which bullying usually is. And I think of the Asian professional whose family lived in a working-class white neighborhood and faced the possibility of running a gauntlet of demeaning name-calling on her way home after school. These children had an innate sense that it would make matters worse to tell adults about their torment, which it probably would have in both cases.

The danger or dread for many others lay at home—sometimes the risk of abuse; sometimes the social risk of classmates knowing what home life is like with a disabled or disheveled parent whose drinking or mental state fluctuates; sometimes the risk of acknowledging a sibling who is not normal. For one girl, it was her mother's emotional callousness toward her love of animals—a story that came out decades later in a women's circle. This woman told us that, while she was at summer camp, her mother gave her dog to the garbage man to get rid of it. She only learned about it when she came home. She knew better than to get upset at her mother, so she buried the incident in her mind and heart. As she remembered it, she sobbed like a child who finally knew it was safe to cry.

In nature, there are predators and prey. The wise child who is vulnerable to predators does what deer, horses, and rabbits do—they blend in with the environment or blend in with the group so as not to draw attention to themselves. Sometimes they freeze and don't move; sometimes they are especially wary at certain times of the day or in certain places. Without having a conceptual understanding of it, children who survive become experts at reading body language, moods, and other signs of what could come next, and also of certain times of the day and certain places. They learn not to show their feelings when it isn't safe to do so; they can and do displace or dissociate from them.

Humiliation, Shame, and Blame

Children feel humiliated when they are treated badly or neglected by adults. They take on the shame adults deserve for what they do or don't do or should do. This psychological reality hurts the heart of the mother bear in me when I hear of it. It is bad enough when what should not happen, does happen; the unfortunate circumstances of natural disasters, war, and illness are part of life and suffering. But unnecessary, egregious suffering is inflicted by adults when a child has to bear the brunt of a parent's alcoholism, misplaced anger, scapegoating, indifference, or jealousy. Children are born good; they want to console or help another crying child or adult. They have an innate sense of justice. So, when they are treated badly or cruelly or neglectfully, they seem to assume they must deserve it. They assume they must be bad, which is compounded by verbal abuse that tells them so. Research done and compiled by Dacher Keltner in *Born to be Good* (2009) presents a convincing case that refutes patriarchal religions and patriarchal psychological theories that say otherwise. Young children want to see their parents as better than they are and are protective of their parents' image at the expense of themselves.

Racism, sexism, and all the "isms" that say that one kind of person is better than another are negative and destructive. And when you are led to believe that you are the "other kind" of child, this has a double negative effect. First you are treated unfairly; then you justify it. I remember a woman who grew up in the deep, segregated South. She was an educated black woman in a professional position in the Bay Area who was reminded by the unusually warm weather in San Francisco about how hot it was when she was a child. She told me that the white kids went swimming in the city pool, but she could not. She justified being excluded by saying what she had been told as a child—that it was necessary because "Negroes are dirty." It hurt my heart that she had internalized this racism and held these prejudices against people who were like her.

Likewise, growing up in any patriarchal culture can result in internalized homophobia in gays and lesbians, and in women who devalue and mistrust other women. In some families, feelings of inadequacy and shame for being female are passed down through generations and, in spite of low expectations, if a girl does well anyway, this counts against her—even when there are no stigmatizing factors. And on top of all these "isms," every girl and woman endures stereotyping and comparison to others and media examples of how women should look. This adds to feelings of inadequacy.

In their teen years, girls who have less-educated or socially or economically less-privileged parents than their classmates—or just parents who are different—can be made to feel shame. This leads to a diminished sense of value, and that judgment sticks until it is acknlowledged and examined. If the parents are immigrants or people who rose out of poverty, they are actually often courageous, hard-working, risk-taking pioneers who made sacrifices to raise their children in America or to send them to college. When you are able to see your childhood and your parents with clarity and compassion, this may restore a sense of worth and give you something of great value: pride in who you are and in your lineage, as well as a new appreciation for the child you were and for your parents.

Much is forgotten and left behind with childhood as we meet the challenges of becoming functioning, respectable adults. Yet, as an adult who was once shamed as a child, you may be susceptible to humiliation and shame, blaming yourself even when it is unreasonable and no fair objective witness would. Perhaps you may remember feeling shame and blame, or recall soul-searing negative words said about you or to you. Instead of others responding with compassion when something painful happens, the tendency is to blame the victim: "*You* must have invited this" or "*you* should have known better . . ."

Seeing the Past in a Different Light

Once you enter the area of recollected feelings and memories of childhood, you have an opportunity to see what happened to you or what you did in a different light. Perhaps you may become a fair witness for yourself—someone who now looks back on those periods of your life when you were shamed or behaved badly, and reappraises them from the perspective of an observing, compassionate, and forgiving adult. You also have an opportunity to appreciate that the child you were had to be brave. You probably were scared and young when whatever shamed you happened—yet you survived. You may have taken your grief and disillusionment out on someone else.

There is healing to be done and a new appraisal to make. Give yourself some credit—you did get through your parents' divorce, or a parent's suicide, or middle school, or the molestation, or family stresses, or the accident, or hospitalization, or the rape—whatever it was that was difficult, maybe even horrible.

When you remember the brave child you once were, consider what was missing then. What can you provide yourself with now? How can you be the adult you wanted at your side—one who loves and applauds, holds and comforts, feels for you but not sorry for you? It was your fate then; now, as an adult, you can be thankful for the child you were. Like a runner who carries the baton in a relay race, or the carrier of the Olympic torch who passes it on, the child you were took the first turn around the track and passed your experiences on to the adolescent, who faced what may have become an obstacle course. Then, from young adult to however old you are now, the cycles of your life continued.

The child who comes into the world with qualities of Artemis can turn to nature and receive much more than temporary shelter from the emotions of others or a place to cry out of sight. It may also have been a place to be curious and happy, to experience awe and wonder. An adult who is moved by nature's beauty and power has received this as a legacy from an Artemis child in her past. The child who is "under the protection of Artemis" keeps her connection to wonder, hope, and courage as she becomes the woman she was meant to be.

The "stuff" of which little Atalanta/Artemis girls are made is not "sugar and spice and everything nice." It is courage in the face of pain and power, or perseverance that keeps up appearances and grades in school, or the resiliency to fall down and get up again. Maybe you were scared and acted as if you were not. Fear did not stop you from stepping up to the challenge of doing something you had never done before and did not know you could do. (This is what societies expect of little boys who are also scared, and young men who are sent to war.) It's having the imagination or inner knowledge that circumstances change and that not all people are like the ones who are oppressing you now. These qualities draw from an unsubdued, untamed spirit that is archetypal. These are qualities that you may have in common with women whose stories I hear in my office, in women's circles, and at the United Nations, where I learned of girls who raise themselves in the midst of armed conflicts, in refugee camps, in lawless cities where they know that they are prey. All were brave girls who held on to hope and became competent and courageous women who share the indomitable spirit of the Artemis archetype.

Some are now women on the front lines of feminism, animal rights, and nature. In their activism, they are like Artemis as the goddess of the hunt, who took action to protect those under her protection and punish those who violated what was sacred to her.

Feminist and mystic have been two sides of my own experience of Artemis as goddess of the hunt and goddess of the moon. Nature is where many of us have had *numinous* experiences—a fitting word, meaning an experience in which we feel awe beyond words for something ineffable, spiritual, mystical—and attribute it to divinity. Such experiences convey a sense of having a place in the universe; of being in a universe that is so vast as to be unimaginable, and yet to matter and have meaning within it. *Gnosis* again: this is not logical, any more than synchronicity and flow or an archetypal dream full of symbols beyond the experience of the dreamer can be explained rationally.

There is another aspect to Artemis as a moon goddess that I now realize comes with living long enough to have an inner psychological sense of the phases of the moon. This comes with my own living through the waxing moon, full moon, and now being well into the waning moon phase of my own life. I still feel outrage and an urge toward action, the two energies that propelled a younger version of me as Artemis armed with her bow and arrows to speak up or do something. The older and wiser version of Artemis is Hecate, the goddess of the waning moon and goddess of the crossroad. It is her counsel that I heed when deciding what I do, now. Is this an old habit—like a Pavlovian response? Or is there vitality and passion in my psyche for this? I'm aware that a goal I am furthering may not be accomplished or resolved in my lifetime, and yet it still matters that I do something to help the eventual outcome. I don't know how the lives of people I love and help will turn out either, and I won't stop loving them.

Lines from Rainer Maria Rilke fit this stage of my life: god is a real, unfathomable source of grace and meaning that I have circled around most of my life. I think of the primordial tower as my *axis mundi* or "the still point of the turning world," to use a phrase from T.S. Eliot's "Burnt Norton."

I live my life in widening circles
that reach out across the world.
I may not complete the last one,
but I give myself to it.

I circle around God, around the primordial tower.
I have been circling for thousands of years,
and I still don't know: am I a falcon,
a storm, or a great song?

PARTING THOUGHTS

Driven as a migrating falcon, I can be blown
off course yet if I turn back it feels
wrong. Navigating by chart and chance
and passion I will know the shape
of the mountains of freedom, I will know.

—Marge Piercy, ending lines of "Perpetual Migration"

You may have been drawn to read this book because you had a sense that it would tell you something about yourself. I hope it has. I also hope that you remember the child you were, and how, with your determination, you survived the difficulties that arose. Nobody gets through childhood scot-free. No parents can protect you from bad things that happen, much less if the bad things that happen are caused by them.

If you recognize Artemis qualities in yourself, chances are that you were a courageous child who probably took some physical risks, did a lot of exploration on your own, and pretended you weren't afraid of or affected by rejection. You persevered; you were called stubborn but would not give up what you believed, although you may have learned to keep quiet about it. You hated seeing defenseless children picked on, or grownups who played favorites or were mean or lied. You may have gotten into trouble for speaking up; you may still be ashamed of yourself for not doing so. The child that you were then still lives in you as your inner child. That child may have carried you through some of the most difficult years of your life, camouflaged whatever you wanted to hide, and managed to hold her head up. You probably have not given much thought to her, unless you have been in therapy.

In therapy and in circles, where people tell the truth of their lives, painful events in childhood and the meaning of them become transformed by a heart-felt response from compassionate and reasonable others—people who say words that you wanted to hear from your parents and those important others who never said them. Words like: "That should not have happened." Or: "They/we should have noticed." Or: "You really did your best." Or: "You are brave." And underlying all these words are the words: "I'm sorry." "You suffered, were not acknowledged." "You matter/ I love you." These are words that acknowledge the suffering and pain that was not allowed expression and the courage it took to bear up. Now, from an adult perspective, you may be able to look back and see yourself, the situation, and the people in a different light. It *is* possible to lift a burden that goes back to childhood and transform it. It *is* possible to be a caring adult to your inner child or to someone else's. It *is* possible for you to forgive and not dwell on what happened that shouldn't have. It *is* possible that you are becoming a compassionate and wise person.

Most of the examples I give here, from Atalanta to real-life stories, are of indomitable girls and women survivors. While every woman, in the course of a lifetime, will have her share of hard times, you may be among the more fortunate or even the most fortunate. Maybe you grew up in a family that loved and supported you to be yourself; maybe you had peers who looked up to you as a leader or athlete or competitor. And maybe you took this all for granted and felt entitled. No one gets through life without suffering. But perhaps now you can realize how lucky you were and probably still are. When you realize just how fortunate you have been, it can move you deeply into gratitude. When gratitude replaces entitlement, this is soul growth.

Recognizing your shadow is humbling. It means remembering and reassessing past experiences, and owning up to hurting or diminishing other people by what you did or said, or what you thought about them. To acknowledge your own lack of compassion or thoughtlessness brings humility and the wisdom that goes with it, which is another lesson in soul growth. Maybe you can make amends to some of these people now, but most of this is inner work.

Anyone who is reading this book is privileged to be educated, literate, psychological, and likely to have an affinity for Artemis. You may have identified with Atalanta and recognize Artemis as a major archetype. You live in a time, a place, and a culture in which this archetype is free to be expressed, as never before in history. If you are drawn to the beauty and mystery of moonlit terrain, which is an aspect of Artemis Goddess of the Moon and of the moon-goddess archetypes, you know something about the liminal, where visible and invisible worlds overlap and words like archetype, angels, and ancestors are meaningful and relevant. This is why you can believe that prayer, mantras, and rituals can have an effect. You may have a sense of an invisible spiritual world when you meditate or pray that connects small self to larger Self, which you also may feel in nature when you are at home there.

Whether you are in an inner-directed phase or an outer-directed one, experiences of the sacred may evoke feelings of love and gratitude and a sense of blessedness in you. This can be a major source of activism-as-giving-back in Artemis-inspired women and men who protect and rescue children and women, who cherish and protect the wilderness, trees, and animals, who nurture the young of all living things, and who believe that men and women should have equal opportunities and responsibilities to shape decisions that matter. When these beliefs enter the mainstream in the world, a new era—as predicted and anticipated by esoteric sources—will come in, making it possible for humanity and the planet have peace and prosper.

I believe that tipping points are reached through one person at a time doing whatever it is that rings true for him or her. Each person is part of a web of consciousness and choice that reverberates and ripples in the invisible human matrix that Jung called the collective unconscious and theoretical biologists call the human morphic field. This interconnection is symbolized by Indra's net, in which each individual is a reflecting jewel at the crossing point of strands on a vast net, and a change in one subtly affects all.

I believe that each of us is also part of an evolutionary journey, a "perpetual migration" toward becoming wise, to live up to our scientific name *homo sapiens* from Latin *sapienta*, meaning wise.

I believe that we are spiritual beings on a human path and that this life we have is a soul journey. From this premise, it matters that we find purpose and meaning in our lives and that we become the women and men we were meant to be.

With the indomitable spirit of Artemis, this effort is best done with love, hope, perseverance, and optimism.

Resources

Mythology

Bulfinch, Thomas. *Bulfinch's Mythology: The Greek and Roman Fables Illustrated.* Compiled by Bryan Holme with an Introduction by Joseph Campbell. New York: Viking Press, 1979,

Callimachus. "To Artemis," in *Hymns and Epigrams.* Translated by A. W. Mair. Cambridge, MA: Harvard University Press, 1969.

Evslin, Bernard. *Heroes, Gods and Monsters of the Greek Myths.* Toronto: Bantam Books, 1968, pp. 173–190. Copyright 1966 Scholastic Magazines, Inc.

Galloway, Priscilla. *Atalanta: The Fastest Runner in the World.* Illustrated by Normand Cousineau. Toronto: Annick Press Ltd., 1995.

Grant, Michael and John Hazel. *Gods and Mortals in Classical Mythology: A Dictionary*. New York: Dorset Press, USA, 1985. First published in Great Britain by Weidenfeld and Nicolson, 1973.

Graves, Robert. *The Golden Fleece*, The Folio Society, 2003. New York: Penguin Modern Classics, 2011.

Hamilton, Edith. *Mythology*. Boston: Little, Brown and Company, 1942. "Atalanta," pp. 244–251.

Mayerson, Phillip. *Classical Mythology in Literature, Art, and Music.* New York: John Wiley and Sons, 1971, pp. 354–357. Atalanta, the Calydon boar hunt and the footrace are in the *Age of Heroes*, written about and staged in the high classical period (fifth century BCE) by Euripides (485–406 BCE) and Aeschylus (525–456 BCE). Mayerson refers to Keats' epic poem *Endymion* often, as well as quoting stanzas from it. Myth details of Selene and Endymion, pp. 166–169.

Miles, Betty. "Atalanta," in Marlo Thomas, *Free to Be . . . You and Me.* Philadelphia: Free to Be Foundation, Inc., 2008, pp. 76–85.

Ovid. *Metamorphoses.* Translated by Rolfe Humphries. Indianapolis, IN: Indiana University Press, 1955, 1983. "The Calydon Boar," pp. 190–195; "The Brand of Meleager," pp. 195–198; "Venus tells the Story of Atalanta," pp. 251–257.

Tripp, Edward. *The Meriden Handbook of Classical Mythology.* New York: New American Library, 1970.

FICTION

Alcott, Louisa May. *Little Women* (1868). Toronto: Bantam Classics, 1983.

Auel, Jean M. *The Clan of the Cave Bear.* New York: Random House, 1980. First of the factually researched series.

Collins, Suzanne. *The Hunger Games.* New York: Scholastic Press, 2008. First of the trilogy.

Gilbert, Elizabeth. *Eat, Pray, Love: One Woman's Search For Everything Across Italy, India, and Indonesia.* New York: Viking Penguin, 2006; New York: Penguin Books, 2007.

James, E. L. *Fifty Shades of Gray.* Australia: The Writer's Coffee Shop, 2011. First of the trilogy.

Larsson, Stieg. *The Girl with the Dragon Tattoo.* Translated from the Swedish by Reg Keeland. New York: Alfred A. Knopf, 2008. First of the trilogy.

Thomas, Marlo. *Free to Be . . . You and Me.* Philadelphia: Free To Be Foundation, 35th Anniversary edition, 2008. Song: "Free to Be You and Me." Music by Stephen Lawrence. Lyrics by Bruce Hart, pp. 10–11.

NON-FICTION

Bolen, Jean Shinoda. *Close to the Bone: Life-Threatening Illness as a Soul Journey,* revised edition. San Francisco: Conari Press, 2007. Originally published New York: Scribner, 1996; paperback edition New York: Simon and Shuster, 1997.

———. *Crossing to Avalon: A Woman's Midlife Pilgrimage.* San Francisco: HarperSanFrancico, 1994.

———. *Goddesses in Everywoman.* San Francisco: Harper & Row, 1984; Harper's Colophon, paperback edition,1985. Thirtieth Anniversary paperback edition (with new Introduction), New York: HarperCollins, 2014. Chapter 3, "The Virgin Goddesses: Artemis, Athena, Hestia"; Chapter 4, "Artemis: Goddess of the Hunt and Moon, Competitor and Sister."

———. *Goddesses in Older Women*. New York: HarperCollins, 2001; paperback edition, New York: Quill, HarperCollins, 2002.

———. *Gods in Everyman*. San Francisco: Harper & Row, 1989; paperback edition, Perennial Library, 1990. Twenty-fifth Anniversary edition with new Introduction, New York: HarperCollins, 2014.

———. *Like a Tree: How Trees, Tree People, and Women Can Save the Planet*. San Francisco: Conari Press, 2011.

———. *Ring of Power: The Abandoned Child, Authoritarian Father, and the Disempowered Feminine*. San Francisco: HarperSanFrancisco, 1992. Paperback edition York Beach, ME: Nicolas-Hays, 1999. New subtitle: *Symbols and Themes, Love vs. Power in Wagner's Ring Cycle and in Us*.

———. *The Tao of Psychology: Synchronicity and the Self*. San Francisco: Harper and Row, 1999. Twenty-fifth Anniversary edition, New York: Harper One, 2004.

Brizendine, Louann. *The Male Brain*. New York: Broadway Books, 2010.

———. *The Female Brain*. New York: Broadway Books, 2006.

Chapman, Marina, with Vanessa James and Lynne Barrett-Lee. *The Girl with No Name*. New York: Penguin Books, 2013.

DeNonne, Donna and Tina Proctor. *Ophelia's Oracle: Discovering the Healthy, Happy, Self-Aware, and Confident Girl in the Mirror*. Golden, CO: Inlightened Source Publishing, 2009. Email reference from Donna DeNomme, quoted with permission.

De Waal, Frans. *The Age of Empathy: Nature's Lessons for a Kinder Society*. New York: Harmony Books, an imprint of Crown Books, 2008.

Downing, Christine. *The Goddess: Mythological Images of the Feminine*. New York: Crossroad Press, 1981. "Artemis: The Goddess Who Comes from Afar," pp. 157–183; "And Now You, Aphrodite," pp. 186–213.

———. *Myths and Mysteries of Same-Sex Love*. New York: Continuum, 1991. "Same Sex Love Among the Goddesses," sections on Artemis and Her Nymphs and The Sacrality of Sexuality, pp. 210–215.

Eisler, Riane. *The Chalice and the Blade*. San Francisco: HarperSan Francisco, 1987.

Ensler, Eve. *In the Body of the World*. New York: Metropolitan Books, Henry Holt and Company, 2013.

Ehrenreich, Barbara. *Living with a Wild God: A Nonbeliever's Search for the Truth about Everything*. Grand Central Publishing, 2014.

Gimbutas, Marija. *The Goddesses and Gods of Old Europe*. Berkeley and Los Angeles: University of California Press, 1982.

———. *The Language of the Goddess*. San Francisco: Harper and Row, 1989.

———. *The Civilization of the Goddess*. San Francisco: Harper and Row, 1991.

Gladwell, Malcolm. *David and Goliath: Underdogs, Misfits, and the Art of Battling Giants*. New York: Little, Brown, 2013.

———. *The Tipping Point: How Little Things Can Make a Big Difference*. Boston: Little, Brown, 2000.

Harding, M. Esther. *Woman's Mysteries: Ancient and Modern*. C. G. Jung Foundation for Analytical Psychology (1971). New York: Bantam Books, published in arrangement with Bantam Books (New York: 1973). "The Virgin Goddess"; Shambala pp.102, 103,125. (1990).

Jung, C. G. *Two Essays on Analytical Psychology*, second edition. Translated by R. F. C. Hull. Bollingen Series 20, Vol. 7, in *Collected Works of C. G. Jung*. Princeton, NJ: Princeton University Press, 1966.

Klinenberg, Eric. *Going Solo: The Extraordinary Rise and Surprising Appeal of Living Alone*. New York: Penguin Books, 2012.

Knox, Jean. *Archetype, Attachment, Analysis: Jungian Psychology and the Emergent Mind*. London: Routledge, 2003.

LeShan, Lawrence. *Cancer as a Turning Point*, revised edition. New York: Plume, a division of Penguin, USA, 1994, p. 23.

Marohn, Stephanie. *What the Animals Taught Me*. Charlotteville, VA: Hampton Roads Publishing Company, 2012.

Miller, Alice. *Prisoners of Childhood: The Drama of the Gifted Child and the Search for the True Self.* New York: Basic Books, 1981.

Neumann, Erich. *Amor and Psyche: The Psychological Development of the Feminine*. Translated from the German by Ralph Manheim. Bollinger Series LIV. New York: Pantheon Books, 1956.

Pert, Candace P. *Molecules of Emotion*, New York: Scribner, 1997, pp. 107–111.

Sandberg, Sheryl. *Lean In: Women, Work, and the Will to Lead*. New York: Knopf, 2013.

Shannon, Lisa. *A Thousand Sisters: My Journey into the Worst Place on Earth to Be a Woman*. Foreword by Zainab Salbi. Berkely: Seal Press/Perseus Books, 2010.

Shephard, Paul and Barry Sanders. *The Sacred Paw: The Bear in Nature, Myth, and Literature*. New York: Viking, 1985.

Singer, June. *Boundaries of the Soul: The Practice of Jung's Psychology*. New York: Doubleday, 1972.

Steinem, Gloria. *Revolution From Within*. Boston: Little, Brown and Company, 1992, p. 37.

Strayed, Cheryl. *Wild: From Lost to Found on the Pacific Crest Trail.* New York: Knopf, 2012.

Switzer, Katherine. *Marathon Woman*. New York: Carroll & Graf Publishers, 2007.

Walker, Alice and Pratibha Parmar. *Warrior Marks: Female Genital Mutilation and the Blinding of Women*. San Diego, CA: Harcourt, 1993. *Warrior Marks*. A film by Pratibha Parmar, 1993.

Willams, Terry Tempest. "Undressing the Bear," in *An Unspoken Hunger: Stories from the Field*. New York: Vintage, 1995.

Yousafzai, Malala. *I Am Malala: The Girl Who Stood Up for Education and Was Shot by the Taliban*. Boston: Little Brown, 2013.

Publications

Als, Hilton. "Bedime Stories: Stephen Sondhiem and James Lapine's Take on Children's Literature," *The New Yorker*, August 27, 2012.

Babu, Chaya. "Girls Choose Better Names," reported from Mumbai, India by the Associated Press, *San Francisco Chronicle,* October 23, 2011.

Baker, Aryn. "Malala Yousafzai, No. 2 Person of the Year," *Time* magazine, December 31, 2012–January 7, 2013.

Brenner, Marie. "The Target" (about Malala Yousafzai), *Vanity Fair,* April 2013.

Deresiewicz, William. "A Man. A Woman. Just Friends?" *New York Times*, April 8, 2012.

Gottlieb, Lori. "The Egalitarian-Marriage Conundrum," *New York Times Magazine*, February 9, 2014.

Htun, Malan and S. Laurel Weldon. "The Civic Origins of Progressive Policy Change: Combating Violence against Women in Global Perspective, 1975–2005," *American Political Science Review*, August 2012.

King, Karisa. "Twice Betrayed," *San Antonia Express-News.* Investigative reporter's seven-month investigation on sexual assault in the military; three-part series published in *San Francisco Chronicle*, beginning May 19, 2013.

Klinenberg, Eric. "Living Alone is the New Norm," *Time* magazine, March 11, 2013.

Newton-Small, Jay. "The Last Politicians," *Time* magazine, October 28, 2013.

Osnos, Evan. "Strong Vanilla: The Relentless Rise of Kirsten Gillibrand," *The New Yorker.* December 16, 2013, pp. 40–45.

Robinson, Roger. "Women's Running Pioneers: Kuscsik, Gorman Honored," *Runner's World*, October 18, 2012.

———. "Courageous Persistence," *Running Times*, October 12, 2012.

Schulz, Connie. "Three Cheers for Pippi!" *Parade* magazine, February 24, 2013, p. 12.

Schwartz, John. "Candace Pert, 67, Explorer of the Brain, Dies," *New York Times*, Science section, September 19, 2013.

Scott, A. O. and Manohla Dargis. "A Radical Female Hero From Dystopia," *New York Times*, April 8, 2012. About Katniss Everdeen in *The Hunger Games.*

Singer, Sally. "Safe at Home: Having Survived a Brutal Sexual Attack, Lara Logan Remains a Tenacious Journalist," *Vanity Fair*, February 2012, p. 161 ff.

Staff article (cover story not attributed). "Gendercide: The Worldwide War on Baby Girls," *The Economist*, March 8–12, 2010, pp. 13, 77–80.

Stein, Joel. "Pixar's Girl Story," *Time* magazine, March 5, 2012, pp. 37–41. About Princess Merida in *Brave.*

Steinem, Gloria. "Our Revolution Has Just Begun," *Ms.* magazine, Winter/Spring 2014.

Talbot, Margaret. "Gone Girl," *The New Yorker*, October 21, 2013. About the abduction of Elizabeth Smart and reference to two others who escaped from captors and wrote books about the ordeal.

Taylor, S. E. , L. C. Klein, B. P. Lewis, R. A. R. Gurung, T. L. Gruenewald, and J. A. Updegraff. "Female Response to Stress: Tend and Befriend, Not Flight or Fight," *Psychological Review*, 2000, pp. 411–429.

Tjaden, Patricia and Nancy Thoennes. "Full Report of the Prevalence, Incidence, and Consequences of Violence Against Women: Findings from the National Violence Against Women Survey," U. S. Department of Justice, National Institute of Justice/Centers for Disease Control, July 2000, publication 183781.

———. "Extent, Nature, and Consequences of Intimate Partner Violence: Findings from the National Violence Against Women Survey," U. S. Department of Justice, National Institute of Justice/Centers for Disease Control, July 2000, publication 181867.

Winnicott Studies, Issue 9. Laurence Spurling, editor. Published for the Squiggle Foundation, London: Karnac, 1994. About Donald Winnicott's idea of "the good-enough mother."

World Development Report 2012. World Bank publication. Quoted by Jeni Klugman.

Online References

Bagby, Rachel. "I am a Full Woman," videotape. *http://vimeo.com*.

Butler, Charles. "40 Years Ago, Six Women Changed Racing Forever," *Runner's World*, October 19, 2012. *www.runnersworld.com*.

Danu, Elizabeth. *www.theliberationofpersephone.com*.

Brave. Disney-Pixar Movies, 2012. *www.movies.disney.com.*

Source of information and documentary filming of bears, mother bear, and newborn cubs in hibernation. *www.covebear.com.*

Huffington, Arianna. "Sarah Palin, 'Mama Grizzlies,' Carl Jung, and the Power of Archetypes," posted August 1, 2010. *www.huffingtonpost.com.*

The Invisible War. Documentary film about sexual assault in the U. S. Military. Written and directed by Kirby Dick, produced by Amy Ziering and Tanner King Barklow, 2012. *http://invisiblewarmovie.com.*

"One Horse Standing," a version of the chant "Bear Metamorphosis." *www.onewhitehorsestanding.com.*

Stolfus, Helen. "Send Word, Bear Mother," documentary. Co-producer and director, Lynn Feinerman. *www.bearmother.com.*

Sloane, Matt, Jasson Hanna and Dana Ford. "Never, ever give up: Diana Nyad completes historic Cuba-to-Florida swim." CNN World, September 3, 2013.

Theoi, Greek mythology. *www.theoi.com.*

Women For Women International: Helping Women Survivors of War Rebuild Their Lives. *http://www.womenforwomen.org.*

Poetry and Music

Bagby, Rachel. "I am a Full Woman," CD, 1993.

Broumas, Olga. "Artemis" from *Beginning with O*. New Haven and London: Yale University Press, 1977.

Piercy, Marge. "The Perpetual Migration" from *The Moon is Always Female.* New York: Knopf, 1980, p. 96–97.

Rilke, Ranier Maria. *Book of Hours: Love Poems to God, ("Widening Circles," I,2).* Translated by Anita Barrows and Joanna Macy. New York: Riverhead Books, an imprint of Penguin Group (USA) Inc., 1996.

About the Author

Jean Shinoda Bolen is a Jungian analyst, psychiatrist, and internationally known author and speaker. She received her medical degree from the University of California School of Medicine San Francisco, interned at Los Angeles General Hospital and did her residency at the Langley Porter Psychiatric Institute, UCSF Medical Center. She is a former Clinical Professor of Psychiatry at UCSF and a Distinguished Life Fellow of the American Psychiatric Association. She is certified in Jungian analysis at the C. G. Jung Institute of San Francisco and is a member of the International Association of Analytic Psychology (IAAP). Bolen is the author of thirteen books that have appeared in eighty-five foreign translations and has contributed to twenty-four anthologies. She is a former board member of the Ms. Foundation, an advocate for a 5th UN World Conference on Women, a convener of the Millionth Circle Initative, and a permanent representative to the UN of the Pathways to Peace NGO. You can find more information on her, and on her books, at *www.jeanbolen.com.*

Index

abandonment, 2, 18, 23, 40–41, 42, 71–72
abductions, 38, 79, 84, 132–133, 196
abortion, 27–28
abuse
  activism against, 126
  blending and vulnerability protection, 18, 209–210
  children and psychological responses to, 210–212
  child sexual, 201–202
  domestic violence, 52–53, 202, 209
  wartime violence against women, 24, 28, 95, 131–132
accomplishment recognition, 79–81, 82
Actaeon, 125
activism
  abuse prevention, 133, 202
  as Artemis archetypal characteristic, 126–130
  bullying, intolerance for, 123, 124, 126, 127
  deforestation protests, 62
  education for girls, 203–205
  gender discrimination, 80–81, 96–97, 148–149
  racial discrimination, 127–128
  sexual assault in military, 81–83
  violence against women, 24, 26, 95–96
  Women's Movement, xiv, 32, 148–149, 176, 193–196
addictions, 191
Africa, 24, 28
Agamemnon, 57
Age of Empathy, The (Waal), 200
Alaska, 33–35
alchemical goddesses, 107, 135. *See also* Aphrodite
Alcott, Louisa May, xii
American Athletic Union (AAU), 96–97
American Psychiatric Association, 148–149
Anastasia Steele, xii
anger, 53–57, 144
anima/animus, 48, 67, 68
animals
  activism protecting, 126
  animal mothers as role models, 14
  child abuse using pets, 209
  as goddess symbols, 15, 53–54, 121–122, 158, 171
  love of, 17–18, 21, 147
  protective strategies of, 18, 209–210
  as surrogate parents, 1, 2–3, 4, 23, 196–201
anti-Semitism, 127

Aphrodite
  as archetypal ally, 153
  associations, 134
  footrace myths featuring, 9, 11, 99, 113
  goddess type, 107, 135
  persona marriages, 113
  reproductive urges, 104
  son of, 159
  virgin goddesses' resistance to, 134
Apollo, 16, 122
Apollodorus, 1
apples, golden, 8–11, 99–108, 157–158
Arab Spring revolts, 22, 131
Arcadia, 1, 2, 8, 90
archetypes. *See also* Artemis archetype
  abandoned child, 40–41, 42
  of Aphrodite, 108, 152
  of Atalanta, 109–110
  of Athena, 134, 136–137, 144, 148–151
  conflicts between, 156–157, 192
  definition and description, 183
  development and configurations of, xiii–xiv, 20, 135, 183–185
  of Hestia, 134, 138
  of men, 110
  motherhood, 104–105
  patriarchy and domestic violence, 53
  of Selene, 160–165
  virgin goddess, 119
Ares, 10, 99
Arethusa, 17
Argonauts, 1, 6, 43–44, 81
arktoi, 15–16
Artemis. *See also* Artemis archetype
  animal symbols of, 15, 53–54, 121–122
  associations, ix, 121
  Atalanta mythology and, 1, 2
  attributes and accessories, ix, xii–xiii, xvi, 16, 122
  companions of, 122
  consequences of offending, 5–8, 51, 53, 60
  descriptions and overview, 121–122
  genealogy of, ix, 16–17, 122
  literature replacing Selene with, 160
  moon symbolism, 153
  protection of, 76–78
  retribution themes, 125–126
  roles of, ix–x, 15, 16–17, 19, 122, 202
  Roman counterpart, ix, 121
  shadow aspects of, 53–54, 144
  vulnerability response of, 147
"Artemis" (Broumas), 74
Artemis archetype
  activism (*see* activism)
  authority issues, 123–124
  concentration and drive, xvi–xvii, 100, 121, 123, 145, 151, 212
  description overview, xv, 148–151
  elusiveness, 53, 121
  ex-spouse relationships, 176
  fictional characters as, xii, xv, 31–32, 122, 123–125, 126
  goddess/mortal combination, 12

grief and healing protection, 73
growing beyond, 146–147
imagination, 21–22, 145
independence and autonomy, 86
love relationships, 136
mother bear protection, 18
mysticism and liminality, 166, 219–220
nature reverence, 16, 76, 121
rage, 53–54, 144
reflection and contemplation, 21, 100, 166
retribution and punishment, 125–126, 144
running, 94
self-determination and journey, 127–129, 187, 188
sisterhood and feminist cause support, 16, 122, 149
tree people, 62
violence survival as non-victims, 130–134
virgin goddess descriptions, 119
woman's life phases for, 11, 202
women as examples of, 20–21, 196–208
Arya Stark, xv
Atalanta
abandonment of, xi, 2, 40
Airtime's protection of, xi, 1, 2
Calydon boar hunt, 5–8, 51, 57–59, 58–59, 67–68
father figures and role models of, 30–32
Hippomenes relationship, 109, 112–113
intimacy issues, 38
life phase correspondence, 156
love and archetypal characteristics of, 109–110
marriage and footrace, classical version, 9–11, 93–94, 98–108
marriage and footrace, modern version, xiii, 114–116, 119
Meleager relationship, 4–5, 10, 47–50, 103
military service, 1, 81
mythology of, 1–12, xi
popularity of, xiii
punishment of, 113
return to Arcadia, 8, 90, 93
tree people archetype, 62
wilderness transition, 8, 72, 79, 87, 89, 90
women's stories compared to, 18, 23, 196–201
Athena, 119, 134, 136–137, 144, 148–151
Atropos, 3, 44
authenticity, 117, 178, 179, 184
autonomy, 86, 156
Ayla (fictional character), xv, 177

babies
birth as transition model, 70–71
desire for, 104–106, 120, 135
gendercide practices, 26–30
identity assumptions and expectations imposed on, 39

maternal care and survival, 44
newborn personalities, 22
patriarchal societies and, 25
Babu, Chaya, 27
Bagby, Rachel, 159
Barrett-Lee, Lynn, 197
bears
cub-rearing descriptions, 13–15
in dreams, 33–36
as goddess animal symbol, 15, 54, 121–122, 171
healing stories and, 32–35
mother bear metaphors, 17–18, 25–26, 126
as mythological surrogate parents, 1, 2–3, 4
women's connection to, 36–38
beauty, attraction to, 160–161, 166
birth, as first transition phase, 70–71, 84
bitterness, 56
blame, 86, 105, 210–212
blending, 18–19, 209–210
bliss, 192–194
boars, 5–8, 51, 53–59, 121, 181
Bones (television show), 49–50
Book of Changes, 85
Born to be Good (Keltner), 210–211
Boston Marathon, 97
boys, 27–28, 39–40, 45–47, 64–66, 73
Brave (movie), 125
Brewer, Heather C., 95
bride prices, 25, 120
Broumas, Olga, 74
Brown, Gordon, 204
bullying, 123, 124, 126, 127, 209, 218
"Burnt Norton" (Eliot), 216

Caesarian sections, 70–71
Callimachus, 122
Calydon boar, 5–8, 51, 53–59, 181
Campbell, Joseph, 192–193
camping, 16, 175
cancer, 78–79, 94–95, 193
Cancer as a Turning Point (LeShan), 193
Capuchin monkeys, as surrogate parents, 23, 197–198, 200–201
Chaos, 159
Chapman, Marina, 23, 196–201, 205
charity events, 94–96
childbirth, ix, 16–17, 70–71, 122
childfree, 105–106, 140
children
abductions of, 132–133
with animals as surrogate parents, 23, 198–197, 200–201, 205
Artemis archetypes in, description, 123–124, 217–218
bullying of, 127, 209
courage and survival of, 208–210
domestic abuse and, 52–53, 201–202, 206, 210–213, 218
education activism and violence against, 203–205, 207

Hestia archetypes in, description, 138
moving frequency and new schools, 129–130
parents' expectations imposed on, 40–42, 63–64
view of parents, 210–211
woman's choice to have, 105–106, 120
Chinese gendercide, 27, 28
Chipko movement, 62
Christianity, 154
circles, women's, 138, 151, 178, 194, 218
Clan of the Cave Bear, The (Auel), xv, 177
Clinton, Hillary, xiv
Close to the Bone (Bolen), 84
collective unconscious, 26
Comeau, Carole, 133
Commission on the Status of Women, 29, 176
compassion, 144–145, 172, 218
concentration, focused, xvi–xvii, 100, 121, 123, 145, 151, 212
conflict of archetypes, 156–157, 192
conformity, 178, 179, 190–192
Congo, 24, 95, 202
coniunctio, 111–112
Constantine, Emperor of Rome, 154
Convention Eliminating Discrimination Against Women (CEDAW), 208
Council of the Thirteen Indigenous Grandmothers, 180
courage, 90, 146, 208–210, 214, 218
crafts, 149
creativity, 89, 106–108, 116–117
crisis, 84
crones (life phase), 138, 139–141, 155, 173, 175, 179–180
Cronos, 38, 137
Crossing to Avalon (Bolen), 88
Cupid (Eros), 159
cycling adventures, 76–77

danger, 84
Danu (Celtic goddess), 78
Danu, Elizabeth, 76–77, 78
Dardenne, Sabine, 132
death and dying, 66–670, 102, 172
Declaration of Sentiments, xiv
deforestation, 62
Demeter, 38, 86, 104, 134, 172, 173
Denali National Park, 33–35
DeNomme, Donna, 19–20
depression, 85, 86
destructive forces, 52–57, 58–62
Devi, Amrita, 62
Diana, 121. *See also* Artemis
Dick, Kirby, 82
dioxins, 33–35
disappearances of women, 28–29
discrimination, 32, 127–130, 148–149, 211–212. *See also* gender discrimination
Disturbing Peace (Havel), 86
divorce, 141, 176–177
does, 121
dogs, 55–57, 171
domestic violence, 52–53, 201–202, 209
dowries, 25, 120

Drama of the Gifted Child, The (Miller), 45
dreams, 32–36, 55–57, 66–67, 155, 159
Duggard, Jaycee, 132

Earth Child Insititute, 95
Eat, Pray, Love (Gilbert), 89
education activism, 203–205, 207
Ehrenreich, Barbara, xviii
Eleusinian Mysteries, 164
Eliot, T. S., 59, 216
elusiveness, 53, 121
emotional development, 45–47, 64–66
emotional experiences, value of, 107
empathy, 38, 111, 136, 144, 145
Endymion, 160–170
Endymion (Keats), 160, 166
Ensler, Eve, 26, 201–202, 206
enthusiasm, 184
entitlement, 54, 219
environmental causes, 60–62, 72, 126
envy, 56
Eos, 160
Eris, 157
Eros, 134, 159, 162
Evslin, Bernard, 2, 47
expectations
  conformity *vs.* authenticity, 178, 179, 190–192
  energy consumption of, 178
  motherhood *vs.* childfree, 105–106
  of parents imposed on children, 40–42, 50, 64
  patriarchal views of marriage, xiv, 109
  time passing and self-imposed, 102
  women in patriarchal societies, 176

fathers, 30–32, 110, 123, 189–190, 201–202
fear, 53, 188, 208–214
female genital mutilation (FMG), 29–30
femicide, 28–29
Feminine, 37
Feminine Mystique, The (Friedan), 105, 176
feminist causes, 16, 122, 126
feminist movements, xiv, 32, 47, 148–149, 176, 193–196
Fifty Shades of Grey (James), xii
Fonda, Jane, 114
footrace mythology, 9–11, 94, 98–99
forgiveness, 144
"For the Fairest," 157
forward thinking, 86–87, 100
Four Quartets (Eliot), 59
Frankl, Viktor, 166
Franklin, Rosalind, 80
freedom, 187–189, 196–201
Free to Be...You and Me (Thomas), xiii, 114, 119–120, 143, 183, 192
Friedan, Betty, 105, 176

Gaia (Mother Earth), 17–18, 37–38, 60, 160
Game of Thrones (Martin), xv
gender. *See also* gender discrimination
  birth ratios, normal, 27
  brain function comparisons, 195–196

patriarchy and marriage roles, 110–111
qualities and roles based on, 111–112
stress management comparisons, 195
gendercide, 26–30
gender discrimination
accomplishment and recognition rejection, 79–81, 82
activism against, 80–81, 96–97, 148–149
conscious-raising movements defying, 32
gendercide practices, 26–28
in Greek mythology, 1, 6, 7, 37–38, 57
healthcare and nutritional neglect, 28
in modern world, 57–58
in patriarchal cultures, 97–98, 109–110, 163, 211
running events and, 96–98
Gilbert, Elizabeth, 89
Gillibrand, Kirsten, 82
Gimbutas, Marija, 24
girls
abductions of, 132–133
courage and survival, xv–xvi, 208–210
education activism and violence against, 203–205, 207
father figures and male role models, 30–32
fictional characters with Artemis archetypes, xv
gendercide practices, 26–30
goddess archetypes of vulnerable, 174–175
goddesses protectors of, 15, 122
healthcare neglect, 28, 44–45
humiliation, shame and blame, 210–214
infancy survival and will, 23
jungle survival, 23, 196–201, 205
missing, 28–29
mother bear parental figures, 17–18
mutilation practices, 29–30
same-sex attractions, 162–163
sexual abuse experiences, 201–202, 206
"Girls Choose Better Names" (Babu), 27
Girl Scouts, 16, 21
Girl with No Name, The (Chapman, et al.), 23, 196–201, 205
Girl with the Dragon Tattoo, The (Larsson), xii, 126
gnosis, 75, 184, 215
god, 215–216
Goddesses in Everywoman (Bolen), x–xi, xiii, 20, 107, 149, 156, 207
Goddesses in Older Women (Bolen), 138, 172
Gods in Everyman (Bolen), 110
Going Solo (Klinenberg), 139–140
Golden Fleece mythology, 1, 43, 81
"Gone Girl" (Talbot), 132
Gonne, Maud, 12

grace, 77–78
grandmothers, 179–180
gratitude, 103, 219
Graves, Robert, 1, 81
Great Goddess (Great Mother), 45, 60, 153–155
Greek culture, ancient, 23–24, 25, 46, 53
Greek mythology. *See also specific names of gods and goddesses*
  abandonment themes, 2, 71–72
  childbirth, 16–17
  gendercide, 2
  gender discrimination in, 1, 6, 7, 37–38
  marriage, 9–11
  military service, 1
  offense of gods/goddesses themes, 51–52, 113
  patriarchy in, 23–24
  rape in, 23–24, 38
Gresham, Zane, 143
grief, 69–70, 71–73, 103–104

Hades, 79
"happily ever after," 116
Harding, M. Esther, 120, 136
hares, 121
Havel, Vaclav, 85–86
healing, 32–36, 69–73, 141, 159, 213
healthcare, and gender discrimination, 28, 44–45
hearth, 137–138, 151
Hecate, 153, 170–175, 180, 215
Helios, 160
Hera, x–xi, 17, 51, 86, 134, 141
Hermes, 9–10, 99
Heroes, Gods, and Monsters of the Greek Myths (Evslin), 2, 47
Hesiod, 1, 159
Hestia, 119, 134, 137–141, 151–152
Hill, Julia Butterfly, 20–21
Hippomenes, 9–11, 99–109, 112–113
homoeroticism, 162
homosexuality, 150, 162, 211
honor killings, 25
hope, 86, 90
horses, 122, 158, 171
Htun, Mala, 194
Huffington, Arianna, 25–26
human trafficking, 17, 25, 29
humiliation, 210–211
humility, 54, 59, 91
The Hunger Games (Collins), 31–32, 122
Hyperion, 160

I Ching, 85
Iliad (Homer), 44
illness, 32–35, 78–79, 84, 94–95, 193
imagination, xi–xii, 21–22, 145
incest, 201–202
independence, 64, 107, 119, 120, 189
India, 26, 27, 28
individuation, 192–193
infanticide, 27–28
infertility, 32–35
Inquisition, 155
inquisiveness, 124
In the Body of the World (Ensler), 201
intimacy, 38, 145–146

Into the Woods (musical), 116
introversion, 137, 138
intuition, 171
Invisible War, The (documentary film), 82
Iroquois Confederacy, 179–180

James, E. L., xii
James, Vanessa, 197
Japanese internment camps, 129
Jason and the Argonauts, 1, 43–44, 57
joy, 187–188, 192–194
judgment, 53, 63–64, 73
Jung, Carl, 25–26, 48, 67, 77, 111, 170, 178
justice, 210, 217–218

Katniss Everdeen, xii, 31–32, 122
Keats, John, 166
Keller, Helen, 220
Keltner, Dacher, 210
Kempusch, Natascha, 132
Kennedy, John F., 41, 176
Kennedy family dynamics, 41
Klinenberg, Eric, 139–140
Klugman, Jeni, 28
Kurgans, 24
Kuscsik, Nina, 97

Larsson, Stieg, xii, 126
leadership, 194–196
Lean In (Sandberg), 116–117, 150–151
LeShan, Lawrence, 193
Leto, 16–17, 122, 171
Liberation of Persephone, The (website), 79
libido, 162, 169
life phases of women. *See also* transition(s)
  first (maiden), 11, 153, 155, 173
  goddess-worshipping societies and, 155
  moon phases as reflections of, 153
  second (full woman/mother), 155, 158–159, 173
  third (crone), 138, 139–141, 155, 173, 175, 179–180, 202
life's journey, 127–130, 185–187
Like a Tree (Bolen), 61, 95
liminality, 171, 176, 219–220
Lindgren, Astrid, 124
Ling, Lisa, 95
lions and lionesses, 121, 171
Lisbeth Salander, xii, 126
Little Women (Alcott), xii
living alone, 139–141
"Living Alone Is the New Norm" (Klinenberg), 140
Living with a Wild God (Ehrenreich), xviii
Logan, Lara, 131–132, 133
loneliness, 85, 140
loss, 69–73, 83–86, 146, 176–177
love. *See also* marriage(s)
  Aphrodite archetypes and, 108
  awareness and importance of, 102–104
  Endymion attractions and obsessive states of, 161–168
  mother's expectations of sons, 63–64

mutual attractions, 168–170
obstacles to, 145–146
as risk, 146–147
solitude and paradoxical synchronicity in, 142–143
virgin goddess archetypes and, 12, 134–135, 136–137, 138
vulnerable goddess archetypes and, 135–136
Luna, 158. *See also* Selene

maidens (life phase), 11, 153, 155
mandalas, 138
marriage(s)
careers and, 116–117
dissatisfaction with, 105
and Endymion attractions, 162, 163
goddesses associated with, 134, 141
Greek mythology on, 9–11, 94, 98, 109, 113, 120
inner *(coniunctio)*, 111–112
in patriarchal societies, 25, 46, 109–111, 120
patriarchal *vs.* egalitarian, 163
persona, 113–114
post-happily ever after of, 116
solitude and paradoxical synchronicity of, 142–143
woman's choices on, 120, 125, 135
maturity, 153, 158
meditation, 138, 139
Meleager
Atalanta relationship with, 4–5, 47–50
birth and early years, 3–4
Calydon boar mythology, 6–8, 62–63, 67–68
death of, 8, 63, 67–68
father's relationship and influence, 42–44, 46
footrace memories of, 10, 100, 103
gender and expectations imposed on, 39
mother's relationship and influence, 44, 45–46, 63–64
memories, 21, 100, 106–107
men
abusive, 37–38, 52–53, 201–202, 209
anima (feminine) psyche of, 111–112
brain function, 195–196
egalitarian attitudes, 110, 163, 196
as father figures and role models, 30–32, 189–190
in leadership roles, 194–195
military service and sexual assault, 81–83
mother's relationship with, 44–47, 63–66
patriarchal power of, 23–26
rage and entitlement of, 54
same-sex attractions, 162
menopause, 138, 155
menstruation, 155
mermaids, 136
Metamorphoses (Ovid), 1, 63
midlife crises, 191–192
midwives, ix, 16–17, 154–155, 171
military service, 1, 81–83
Millennium series (Larsson), 126

Miller, Alice, 45
Millionth Circle initiative, 178, 194
monkeys, as surrogate parents, 23, 197–198, 200–201
moon, 21, 153, 155. *See also* moon goddesses
moon goddesses, xviii, 21, 100, 121, 153, 219–220. *See also* Artemis; Hecate; Selene
moonstruck/mooning, 161–162
mother (life phase), 153, 155
mother bears, 13–15, 17–18, 25–26, 33–36, 121, 126
motherhood
  animals as role models for, 13–15
  Artemis archetype and, 135
  decisions regarding, 104–106, 120, 135
  emotional bonds, 38, 64–65
  Greek mythology themes of, 37–38
  as humility and sacrifice, 147
  maternal care and infant survival, 44–45
  one-in-herself *vs.*, 147
Mother Nature/Mother Earth (Gaia), 17–18, 37–38, 60, 160
mothers
  goddesses associated with, 134
  indomitable spirit support *vs.* suppression, 189–190
  relationship with sons, 44–47, 63–66, 68
  responsibility and blame for children, 22–23
Murray, W. H., 200
mysticism, 164, 166, 214–215
My Story (Smart), 132

Native American cultures, 179–180
natural disasters, 51, 60
nature
  activism protecting, 60–62, 72, 126
  Artemis archetype and, 16, 21, 73–77, 76
  destruction of, 180–181
  destructive forces of, 51, 60
  healing in, 72–76, 213–214
  outdoor challenges, xvi–xvii, 16, 73–77, 175
New York City Marathon, 96–97
Nietzsche, Friedrich, 133
Nobel Peace Prizes, 80, 203
non-victims, 130–133
Nyad, Diana, xvi
nymphs, 122

Odyssey, The (Homer), 174
O'Keeffe, Georgia, 89
Oliver, Mary, 70
One Billion Rising, 26, 201, 206
one-in-herself
  fullness and maturity as, 158–159
  as intimacy and vulnerability obstacle, 145
  introversion and, 137, 138
  love relationships, 134–135
  marriage/motherhood and, 120, 147
  for non-victim survival, 132
  as virgin goddess characteristic, xviii, 119
opportunity from loss, 84

opposites, attraction of, 112
Ovid, 1, 63, 113

Palin, Sarah, 25–26
parents
  abusive, 52–53, 201–202, 208–212
  children neglected by, 18, 21, 44–45
  child's view of, 210–211
  expectations imposed on children by, 39–42, 50
  father figures as role models, 30–32
  patriarchal roles and expectations of, 109
  son's love choices and judgment of, 63–64
  support or suppression of spirit, 189–190
  women as mother bears, 17–18, 25–26
Paris, 157
Parmar, Pratibha, 30
passion, 165–166, 169
patriarchy
  Athena archetypes and, 149–150
  attractions, view of, 162, 163
  authenticity suppression and, 189
  boys and grief expression, 73
  decision-making roles in, 157
  description, 24
  gender discrimination, 211
  in Greek culture and mythology, 23–24, 25, 46, 53
  marriage conventions, 25, 46–47, 94, 109–111
  in Middle East, 25, 207–208
  motherhood roles in, 37–38
  obedience requirements, xiv, 97–98
  religion and, 153–154
Peleus, 58
"Perpetual Migration, The" (Piercy), 185, 217
Persephone, 38, 79, 84, 86–87, 134, 172, 173
perseverance, 78–79, 189
persona marriages, 113
personas, 191
Pert, Candace, 80–81
Piercy, Marge, 185, 217
pilgrimages, 34, 88–89, 177
Pippi Longstocking, 124
Pluto, 107
Poseidon, 51
poverty, 211–212
power, 40–41, 187–188
pregnancy, 32–36, 154, 155
Princess Merida, 125
Procrustean process, 190–191
Providence, 200
Psyche, x, 159
punishment, 52–53, 113, 125–126, 144

quail, 53, 121

racism, 127, 129–130, 209, 211
rage, 52–62, 144
rape
  child sexual abuse, 201–202
  as family dishonor, 25
  goddesses as protectors from, 1, 17, 122, 130
  in Greek mythology, 23–24, 38

international statistics, 130
in military service, 81–83
non-victim response to, 130–134
vulnerability and, 19–20
as warfare tactic, 24, 95
Reason in Common Sense (Santayana), 71
recognition, 79–81, 82
reflection, 21, 100, 101–102
refugees, internally displaced, 129–130
rejection, 79–81, 90, 136, 145. *See also* abandonment
religions, matriarchal *vs.* patriarchal, 153–155
remorsefulness, 59
retribution, 54, 125–126, 144
revenge, 86, 130
Rhea, 38, 137
Rilke, Rainer Maria, 215–216
Ring Cycle (Wagner), 41
Ring of Power (Bolen), 40–41
Robinson, Carole, 142–143
romance, 49
Roman mythology, 107, 121, 158
Rumi, 166
Run for Congo Women, 96, 127
Run for the Cure, 94–95
running, 94–98, 100, 127

Sandberg, Sheryl, 116–117, 150–151
Santayana, George, 71
"Sarah Palin, Mama Grizzlies, Carl Jung, and the Power of Archetypes" (Huffington), 25
Schulz, Connie, 124
Selene, 153, 158–170
Self, 37, 56, 77, 178
self-determination, 127–129, 187, 188
self-sufficiency, 21, 103
Send Word, Bear Mother (film), 32–35
Seneca Nations, 179–180
seventh generation principles, 179
sexism, 32, 211
sexual attraction, 162
shame, 190, 210, 211–213
Shannon, Lisa, 95–96, 127
sisterhood, 16, 122, 149–150
Smart, Elizabeth, 132–133
Smith, Patricia, 196
snakes, 171
solitude, 138, 139–141
Sondheim, Stephen, 116
sovereignty, 139–141, 196–200
stags, 53, 121
Steinem, Gloria, 18–19, 20, 47, 110, 149, 206–207
Stevens, Onnolee "Onzie," 175–176, 178–179
Stoltzfus, Helen, 32–35
Strayed, Cheryl, 73–76
suicide, 19
support, 172
swimming challenges, xvi–xvii
Switzer, Kathrine, 97
synchronicity, 77–78, 200

Talbot, Margaret, 132
Taliban, 203–205
Tao of Psychology, The (Bolen), 21, 77
Terence, 107
Teresa of Avila, 166
Theia/Thea, 160

Theogony (Hesiod), 159
Thomas, Marlo, xiii, 114, 119–120, 143, 183, 192
Thousand Sisters, A (Shannon), 96
"Three Cheers for Pippi!" (Schulz), 124
time passing, 101–102
Tiresias, 174
Titans, 158, 160, 171
tomboys, 15–16
toxins, 32–35
transition(s)
of Atalanta, 8, 72, 79, 87, 89, 90
birth as first, 70–71
causes of, 69, 70, 83–84
crisis and, 84
divorce and survival, 176–177
goddesses associated with, 171–172
wilderness metaphors for, 69–76, 83–91
women's life stages in, 152
travel, 88–89
trees and tree huggers, 60–62, 72, 126
Trinity, 154
Triple Goddess (Great Mother), 45, 60, 153–155
Trojan War, 157
twinning, 47–50

underworld mythology, 84–85, 107, 173–174
Unspoken Hunger, An (Williams), 36–37
"unwanted" girls' name translations, 27
Uranus, 37–38, 160

Vagina Monologues, The (Ensler), 202, 206
victimization, 19, 28, 130–133
violence against women. *See also* rape
domestic violence, 52–53
education activism and, 203–205, 207
non-victim response to, 130–134
wartime, 24, 28, 95
Violence Against Women Act, 17
virgin goddesses. *See also* Artemis; Athena; Hestia
archetypal characteristics of, xviii, 107, 119, 134, 148–152 (*see also* Artemis archetype)
as non-victims, 130
shadow aspects of, 144–146
virginity, xiv, 1, 25, 29–30, 122
Virgin Mary, 154
virgins, psychological, 119, 120, 132
vulnerability
Artemis' response to, 147
exposure of, as act of courage, 90
of love, 136, 167–168
obstacles to, 145
revelation and victimization, 19
shadow aspects overcome by, 144, 145
survival tactics and hidden, 18–19, 209–210
vulnerable goddesses, 86, 107, 135–136. *See also* Demeter; Hera; Persephone

Waal, Frans de, 200
Wagner, Richard, 41
Walker, Alice, 30
war, 24, 28, 96, 131–132, 202
Warrior Marks (Walker and Parmar), 30
Weldon, S. Laurel, 194
Wild (Strayed), 73–76
wilderness, 8, 69–76, 79, 83–91
"Wild Geese" (Oliver), 70
William, Prince of England, 40
Williams, Terry Tempest, 36–37
"wind under her wings," 77
Winnicott, Donald W., 22
wisdom, 149, 155, 172, 173–175
witches, 155, 171
Woman's Mysteries (Harding), 120, 136
women. *See also* gender discrimination; girls; rape
  animus (male aspect) of, 111–112
  brain function, 195–196
  domestic violence statistics, 52, 53
  full, 158–159
  goddess-worshipping societies and status of, 154–155
  leadership roles, 194–196
  patriarchal roles and expectations of, xiv, 37–38, 46–47, 97–98, 109–110, 163
  pre-feminist era roles, 176–177
  as wartime collateral damage, 24, 28, 95
Women in the Congo, 95
Women's Movement, xiv, 32, 47, 148–149, 176, 193–194
Women's Suffrage Movement, xiv
Women to Women International, 95
Wonder Woman, 124
Woodman, Marion, 70–71
World Conference on Women, xiv, 17, 150, 193

Xena the Warrior Princess, 125

Yeats, William Butler, 12
Young John, 115–116, 119
Yousafzai, Malala, 203–205, 207–208

Zeus
  Endymion myth, 160
  footrace prayers to, 10
  genealogy and family, 16–17, 38, 122–123, 137
  opera characters comparisons, 41
  patriarchal roles of, 53, 154
  violence of, 24, 51

About Conari Press

Conari Press, an imprint of Red Wheel/Weiser, publishes books on topics ranging from spirituality, personal growth, and relationships to women's issues, parenting, and social issues. Our mission is to publish quality books that will make a difference in people's lives—how we feel about ourselves and how we relate to one another. We value integrity, compassion, and receptivity, both in the books we publish and in the way we do business.

Our readers are our most important resource, and we appreciate your input, suggestions, and ideas about what you would like to see published.

Visit our website at *www.redwheelweiser.com* to learn about our upcoming books and free downloads, and be sure to go to *www.redwheelweiser.com/newsletter* to sign up for newsletters and exclusive offers.

You can also contact us at *info@rwwbooks.com*.

Conari Press
an imprint of Red Wheel/Weiser, llc
665 Third Street, Suite 400
San Francisco, CA 94107